RUNNING THE FOUR-MINUTE MILE AND OTHER DELUSIONS

A.J. SCHMITZ

Confessions of a
Second-Rate Athlete

MAXIXAM
PRESS

Stephen

Run like the wind

Everything in this book is true.

Some of the names have been changed
to protect me from running my mouth.

Contents

Part 1

Running the Four-Minute Mile

1

It started with a dream.

Doesn't it always?

Not a sleeping dream where I jolted from the bed in a twisted knot of sheets and shouted, YES!

It was a daydream at first.

Tucked between visions of being the New York Jets general manager, a job I *know* I can do better than the current general manager, and being the New York Knicks head coach, a job I now realize I *cannot* do better because I'm the coach of my son's basketball team and we haven't won a game yet, was my realistic dream.

A dream about running.

First and foremost, I understand my limits of coaching basketball, mainly because the parents of my son's teammates *also* think they're a coach and freely dispense advice to me on how to run the team, none of it useful as these kids are not Magic Johnson and Larry Bird, if you can believe that.

Secondly, I know most male adults between the ages of 22 and 75 believe they can do a better job drafting players and building a football team better than the New York Jets organization, yet none of them, including me, will ever have that opportunity, so we're left with our smaller dreams.

Right now, my dream is running.

The famous Chicago Bulls basketball coach Phil Jackson says in his book *Sacred Hoops* that through the teachings of the Lakota Native Americans, and through his own experience, that "the expansive dream state [is] where everything begins, and all is possible." I'm not Lakota Native American or Phil Jackson, but that's a philosophy I can get behind.

I tend to daydream about all sorts of strange and unattainable goals… concert pianist, Lego Master Builder, dog show groomer, and bodyguard to famous actors. Some of these dreams are possible if I could "just get away from this damn computer," the same computer I use to make a living. While I was in the middle of creating a social media post for a non-profit's wine-tasting event, I shelved the more unrealistic goals of being responsible for the roster of a billion-dollar sports franchise and focused on running fast. That was something that required nothing more than walking out the door wearing athletic sneakers.

This daydream came one day about two years ago when I ran really fast because I was terribly late for a meeting. I said to myself: "How hard is it to run a four-minute mile? Seems fairly easy. I mean, one lousy mile? I must walk 10 or 20 miles a day just living life; surely, I can turn up the speed and hit one mile in a matter of seconds." The more the idea jogged my brain, the more I realized it was harder than expected.

Of the many hurdles I encountered during the start of this dream, was math.

I know what you're thinking…

"math, something you do with your brain, shouldn't stop you from running, something you do with your legs," but believe me, it did.

I went to a local high school track just to get the feeling of being there and let me tell you, I immediately wanted a tall coffee at some sleepy cafe and watch the people go by. I'd been going to the gym for years, but running on hard clay (or the hard rubber particle stuff the track was molded into) was way less satisfying than I thought. Not only that, it was something in the range of 20 degrees Fahrenheit outside. My breath turned to ice crystals right before my very eyes. I should have waited till spring, but my interest was right then and there. The math part came when I didn't know what a mile was on the track. How many times do I need to run around the track the hit a mile? One? 14? I didn't know. I pulled out my phone and Googled the answer. Goggle didn't tell me. I must have rephrased the question 10 times.

"How many times do I need to run a track to hit a mile?"

"How many rotations do I need to go around a high school track to make a mile?"

Nothing came up. I decided at the very least to look for the answers on the track itself. There are numerous lines, markings, starting and ending points all over the place. I know from watching the Olympics the lines are staggered for the starter blocks because the outside track is longer than the inside track. That's the math right there. But the more I looked at the confounding lines and numbers on the track, the more frustrated I became.

To quell that frustration, I simply began to run. I did ONE measly lap around the track, and I nearly died.

Okay, not died, but I almost hurled my breakfast.

I know, not a great start.

I probably should have consumed a lighter breakfast, having scoffed down an omelet and a massive coffee, but this was a learning process. Most runners eat foods like almond milk with berries and tree leaves. Foods animals living on sheer mountainsides eat. Runners are also svelte; lean like gazelles with their muscles at the surface of the skin, pulsating like a million rubber bands twisting on a rubber band machine. I've never actually seen a rubber band machine, but you know what I mean... we can assume the rubber bands are stretched and twisted to test their elasticity. These rubber bands need to be used to secure rolled-up drawings, to fascine small boxes, and to fling at the heads of fellow students during study hall. But I digress. You get my point.

I, on the other hand, was not stringy, but rather soft. Sure, I had some fine muscles having worked myself into decent shape at the gym. But was I lean and elastic like the long-distance runner? Nope. Not even close. In fact, I got winded walking up the stairs to go to bed. Good thing I was going to bed because I was wiped out!

Running isn't just the muscles used to fling the arms and legs around, the body needs a high-functioning cardiovascular system as well. That's essentially everything inside your body... lungs, heart, veins and I assume all your internal organs on some level. Those things need to be high functioning along with the limbs, and mine were most certainly not. So, I did what everyone training to run a four-minute mile would do. I ignored that dream and did nothing for two years.

2

Let me be clear, I didn't do *nothing* for the entire two-year stretch. I did some serious research. I went to the internet to see how many people have broken the four-minute mile.

I figured since it's such a monumental achievement, it must only be a handful of superior athletes. Maybe somewhere in the vicinity of 40 or 50 people. But it's not. There's a lot of people who've run a sub four-minute mile. Roughly 1,800 of them. Some of them legends of the sport. Household names like Yomif Kejelcha and Hicham El Guerrouj. Men whose faces line the walls of teen athlete bedrooms next to Michael Jordan and Tom Brady. I'm kidding. Nobody knows these people! But they're known in the running world.

I realized I wouldn't get legendary status running a four-minute mile. Perhaps I could be the OLDEST person to run a four-minute mile. I researched what old geezer holds the record and it's an Irishman by the name of Eamonn Coghlan. He was 41 when he did a sub four-minute mile. I was 51 at the time of this research. That's a full decade older if you can do math. Not only that, Eamonn was one of those lean, wiry types – built like a spider monkey with lungs more expansive than weather balloons, able to push oxygen into the blood-stream faster than a junky pushes heroin into the vein. That info felt defeating, but I wasn't crushed. Not yet.

The crush came when I did math.

Yes, that damn math again!

I wasn't a good student in school and math is my kryptonite, but I can do basic math to figure out a tip at a restaurant, or the correct coins to hand a cashier for the purchase of a bag of chips.

By my calculations, a person must run 15 miles-per-hour to beat a four-minute mile. That was confirmed when I Googléd the question and was given the answer in 5 seconds. *Now* Google helps me out with an answer!

I don't know if you realize this, but 15mph is really *really* fast.

For a human.

Biologically, we're not an efficient animal. Throw some humans onto a basketball court or on a football field and we excel. I mean, we obviously invented those games, so a cat or a dog can't excel at them, but a cat and a dog can bolt pretty damn fast. Humans cannot. The average top speed of most humans is around 12 miles per hour. So, running 15mph for a solid four miles is quite the challenge. I can't even play a video game for four minutes without my thumbs screaming in agony, so using my entire body to run at top speed for four minutes around a hard rubber track felt like nothing short of impossible.

But I was determined.

I told my wife Rita about the four-minute mile and its illustrious history. She had no idea what I was talking about. None. She thought a four-minute mile was easy. She's worse at math than me!

Actually, that isn't true because she might be a math genius. One day she and my son were tossing numbers around to add together, and Rita was doing it without batting an eye. When they hit the triple digits and her powers of addition continued unabated, we knew she was special. Regardless, her lack of enthusiasm over this difficult running achievement left me crestfallen. I told her if I was to try this feat, I'd need to run 15 miles-per-hour for four minutes without stopping and her response was to shrug her shoulders and fork a twisted ball of spaghetti into her mouth. It was obvious she would not be my motivation in this process.

She was the one who suggested long ago that I needed to do "more cardio" at the gym, and I said, "yeah, I guess you're right" and I parlayed that suggestion into conquering the hardest achievement in running. But that's just how I roll... like an idiot.

After years of mulling this thing in my noggin' it was finally time to take this four-minute mile thing seriously. And it was technology that would help me do it... in more ways than one.

First, technology helped to educate me on how many rotations I'd need to traverse the track to hit a mile. The answer was four. No, it wasn't Google that gave me the answer, it was the treadmill at the gym.

Finally, the treadmill was good for *something*!

It had a little track on the monitor, and when I ran, the area I covered would fill with a nice cobalt blue color, which was incredibly satisfying.

Second, the treadmill would also be the equipment I'd use to get in four-minute mile shape. I wanted to use the regular *ordinary* world to train… like the filthy streets of my 'hood while lifting household items like a dishwasher over my head… but the treadmill and the gym's comfortable, highly advanced equipment would have to do.

I had visions of a montage where I would run through the mountains in waist high snow and fight mountain lions to achieve the level of physicality needed to run this mile. Like Rocky Balboa did in *Rocky IV*. If you don't remember, or have not seen that masterpiece of 1980's American filmmaking, Rocky trains on the hills of Siberia (or somewhere) and runs in the snow, rolls large rocks around, chops wood, and lifts up his wife and trainer in a giant wheelbarrow (don't ask) to hone his body into the boxing machine needed to defeat a lab-grown master race cyborg by the name of Ivan Drago. If you don't shed at least one tear at the climax of this film, you don't have a soul, and you're most certainly not an American who enjoys guns, ammo, and American eagles flying over flapping flags of stars and stripes.

My first go at the four-minute mile was shaky at best.

I clocked in at *just* over four minutes with the time of 16 minutes and 38 seconds. That's like… 45 minutes over the four-minute mark.

Listen, I told you I wasn't good at math.

Was I defeated by these numbers? Heck, no! I knew it would be a grind, and I was in this to win this, so I understood my poor time was just the start. The beginning. The starting line, so to speak. Would Rocky quit? Of course not! I mean, he's quit roughly six or seven times during the run of the franchise's six or seven films, but that's the point of Rocky's story. He feels defeated, quits, then someone gives him an incredible pep talk about life, his legacy, or his wife who's currently in a coma, and it wakes him from the mental pit he's fallen into. Sometimes it's the trainer giving the speech... sometimes it's his actual wife (out of the coma of course). Some of these motivational speakers have died in the middle of giving him this pep talk, and that event *in itself* has motivated him to decapitate his opponent in the ring. I don't need, and I certainly don't want, that type of motivation. I'd like everyone in my life to be alive and healthy, so the inner fire of motivation needed should be lit from within – by me.

I really upped my enthusiasm for the second go at the four-minute mile. I clocked in at 14 minutes and 12 seconds. I shaved a full... 30 minutes off my time.

Again, math.

But I could see the improvement. I celebrated by eating an entire meatball hero for dinner that night.

Then I figured Eamonn Coghlan (old Irish dude) isn't eating meatball heroes for dinner because he's built like a man who eats air for dinner, then runs a marathon immediately after, so portion control and healthier choices were needed to improve stomach performance, which in turn helps the lungs and limbs. They say: "the stomach is the way to a man's heart," but I think that's a philosophy about the ways of love. In terms of four-minute miles, the *heart* is most likely the way to the heart in the physical sense. You don't want the heart exploding in your chest, so proper diet and a good dose of exercise is the way to get the ticker tocking correctly.

Another issue I had after my second run on the treadmill was muscle tightness. I'm very good about stretching. My son plays basketball, and I stress the importance of stretching because flexibility prevents injuries and can lengthen the athlete's longevity. For some reason I didn't stretch enough before running and my calves began to ache... as well as my Achilles tendons... and my thighs... and my knees... and my lungs, feet, heart and head. But other than that, I felt great!

So, on my next go around, I stretched to prevent aches, ate only a small banana as fuel, and for motivation, envisioned Eamonn Coghlan crying in the corner of his trophy room, having his record shattered by someone 10-*something* years older than him. The results of this discipline were immediately apparent.

My third run time under the umbrella of my new objective came the very next day after my second run. It was a disappointing result. 14 minutes and 28 seconds. I did *worse*. But these things happen. You know; two steps forward, one step back. It's a good analogy because it involves feet which one uses to step *and* to run, but this stepping analogy is universal as an example of progress and regression, whether one uses their feet or not.

I admit, I was a bit tired after my grueling mile the previous day. My left ankle hurt and stiffened up, even though I stretched longer than day two. I attacked the third run with vigor, bursting with speed at the start and circumnavigating the first lap in about 3 minutes. After that, my afterburners ran out of fuel. I began to hobble like a pirate running on a peg leg. My average for each track rotation went from 3 minutes, to over 4 minutes. Those who can do math better than me will notice that going around the track once in four minutes will not break the record when I need to circle the track four times in four minutes. My time went longer and my dream of getting under the four-minute mile drifted further into the distance.

Zeroing in on the treadmill's monitor, the blue oval began to resemble a cheery, yet twisted smile as it mocked my failure to achieve my goals in more ways than one. A giant U that eventually formed a 0. A big, fat 0!

I've seen YouTube videos where people who are upwards of 300 pounds claim they're going to run a marathon and I think "yeah right!" and by the end of the video, they've accomplished that goal. They not only lost the weight but got into marathon shape. Not so easy to achieve. I feel stupid for doubting them. Cruel even. Who am I to judge? One time I was too lazy to reach for the TV remote, so I used a chicken leg to pull the remote closer to me. When the channel didn't change to the football game because the batteries were dead, I watched bull riding. BULL RIDING! I ate chicken legs and watched men in cowboy hats bounce on wild beasts while a playoff football game was on another channel. These YouTube video people found the motivation to run 26.3 miles because that was their dream. I found inspiration in that. I too had a dream. To run the four-minute mile and do it without needing a knee transplant.

Speaking of knees, there was this guy Terry Fox who had one leg, and this guy found the motivation to run across Canada for charity. He ran on a prosthetic leg and hobbled across Canada. He also ran the New York City marathon. He was quoted as saying "I just wish people would realize that anything's possible if you try, dreams are made if people try."

Fine words indeed.

Still, looking at the overall picture of things, my motivation was low. I didn't have someone like Johnny Walker to yell in my face, and I don't mean the whiskey, although whiskey has motivated many people to do many things, most of them stupid and not resulting in broken records but mostly broken backs, broken homes and broken promises. I needed 1976 Olympic gold medalist Johnny Walker to yell in my face. I needed an old, gruff trainer with a crooked mouth to insult me and tell me how worthless I was. I needed someone to challenge me. A partner. A competitor. So, I contacted my buddy, Stephen.

Stephen is the kind of guy who listens to running podcasts, reads books about running, and of course – runs! He runs marathons and sometimes travels to different parts of the world to run marathons. He runs at night, runs in the rain, and he runs at the crack of dawn. You know? Things INSANE people do. But he's motivated. He keeps those number tickets marathoners wear on their chest and sticks them to his walls, and he has his finishing times taped to the refrigerator with his kid's drawing. He has photos of himself and his friends sweating all over each other at the marathon finish line, looking as if they were just released from a hostage situation. There's also pictures of them drinking beer afterwards. Apparently, beer after a marathon is a thing and if that's the case, call me a runner. If you can't win the gold medal, at least enjoy a golden beer.

Stephen has talked about books to read like *Born To Run*, which I was disappointed to find out was NOT about Bruce Springsteen, but about a guy named Christopher McDougall who researched all the ways we run – the history of running, the tribes of the world who consider running sacred, people who run without shoes, and all sorts of things. I didn't really research this book at all, these are things I believe Stephen told me years ago. He also told me this while we were drinking beer, and although I've discussed beer as being something invigorating to consume after you've abused your body with running, it's not recommended to drink if you're trying to remember past discussions about running books.

Here's how that inspirational text message exchange between Stephen and I went down.

Me: *"Hey, I'm trying to be the oldest person in the world to run a four-minute mile"*

Stephen: *"haha"*

3

My next task on my journey to the four-minute mile was to watch a seminal 1980s running film.

I know what you're thinking. "Do you do anything but watch 1980s movies?"

The answer is yes; I watch 1990s movies as well. Have you seen *Demolition Man* with Sylvester Stallone? It's no *Rocky IV*, but it's a dang good movie. Not a lot of running in it, but it's clever. Arnold Schwarzenegger made a movie called *The Running Man* in 1987 (sorry, back to the 80s) and although there isn't a lot of running in that movie, running is in the title, so titles can be deceiving. There's a new *Running Man* movie coming out in a few months as of this writing, which may have more running than the first movie. *Forrest Gump* is a 1990s movie and at one point he runs back and forth across the country a bunch of times, which is crazy, but Forrest wasn't exactly the sharpest chocolate in the box. In *Rocky I*, which back in the day was just *Rocky* because they hadn't made the endless sequels, he runs a lot. It's part of his training. He eats a cage-load of raw eggs and runs in the streets while the garbage men are hauling away Philadelphia's putrid trash. He also runs after a chicken, but not for the eggs because those were in his refrigerator. He runs after the chicken to increase his speed. At first Rocky can barely run, mainly because he smokes cigarettes, but later, he manages to get to the Philadelphia Museum of Art without puking his guts out. I don't smoke, so I have that advantage, but I can't say I'm in better shape than Rocky was.

I also watch 1970s movies as well.

There's *Marathon Man*, *Silent Running*, and *Logan's Run*, none of them about people running for their health and training for the four-minute mile. That movie is Academy Award-winner for Best Film *Chariots of fire* (1981). Yes, this film beat out *Raiders of the Lost Ark* to win best picture, a tragedy that has yet to be rectified. Think about it; how many times have you talked about *Raiders* and how many times have you talked about *Chariots* in the past 40 years?

Yeah, that's what I thought.

Anyway, this might be the only time in my life when *Chariots of Fire* is important to me. If I must confess, I've never actually watched *Chariots of Fire*, so my past claims to it being significantly less important than *Raiders* in the lexicon of film history may be overblown. I could never figure out how a movie about running could be entertaining as well as being the finest film of that particular year. They're running. Running is boring. Watching people run is even MORE boring. Still, they've made some fantastic movies about boring subjects... chess with *Searching for Bobby Fischer* and Jazz drumming with *Whiplash*. Yet, I've been to the New York City Marathon multiple times and it was dreadfully boring. I had no choice to be there because every November, the marathon ran right past my apartment window on first avenue in Manhattan. They don't let you cross the street on the off chance you'll get runover by a mob of delirious runners stumbling forward like those people falling down hill in that famous Cooper Hill Cheese Rolling contest that has fractured more legs and opened more skulls than your average multi-vehicle highway crash. The NYC Marathon forced me to retire to my apartment and drink beer, which is a beverage we've discussed far too many times already.

There's also a 1960s movie that was first a book from 1959, titled: *The Loneliness of the Long Distance Runner*. I don't know what the story was about, but *of course* he was lonely. He's running a *long distance*. No one wants to run long distances with a long-distance runner, and if they try, they eventually drop out. They say: "screw it, this guy isn't going to stop, he's running a long distance." So, they drop out and do something involving a shorter distance. Like running a four-minute mile. You *know* how long that event will take because it's literally in the title of the activity. Four minutes? Sounds great! Count me in. I'll run four minutes, and the other 23 hours and 56 minutes of the day can be spent doing something meaningful – like daydreaming about being the director of a bigtime Hollywood movie whose subject matter will be infinitely more interesting than running.

Eventually, I sat down for my first watch of *Chariots of Fire*, hoping for enlightenment, motivation, and to be assured Steven Spielberg and George Lucas were robbed of golden Oscar statuettes.

The film opens briefly on a funeral, then cuts to the iconic and charming scene of men dashing and splashing through beach surf to the plinking Oscar-winning film score by Vangelis, who later did the iconic music for the film *Bladerunner*, another film about running, except that's about humanoids being run down and executed in cold blood by police hunter Harrison Ford, who coincidentally was in *Raiders of the Lost Ark*, the film *Chariots of Fire* robbed of an Oscar. The parallels are eerie.

Immediately I sense the film will be a stuffy British drama filled with crew neck sweaters and glacial pacing to the point of deep boredom. The undertones of antisemitism leak early, letting me know this film will be about more than running. During a college class registration, the chaps, particularly Harold Abrahams, do a 60 second sprint for sport where they immediately celebrate the success (or maybe they broke a record) by popping a bottle of champagne. The film immediate rises in stature in my eyes. 60 seconds of exercise capped by a bottle of champagne is a ratio I can appreciate. Personally, that kind of hedonism won't do in terms of speed training, but the sentiment is there.

Another observance during the film's early start is there will most likely be absolutely no chariots of fire. I knew this was a historical film, but apparently not Ancient Rome. It takes place in Scotland in the early 1920s, a fine place and time, but no chariots. I realized the chariot thing was more a metaphor, which is fine, but chariots are pulled by horses while the people ride *inside* the chariot part, so I'm not sure who was dispensing the metaphors, but they should have been run out of town.

The film has multiple points of views. Pompous head-masters, pompous classmates.... Even the people who are not pompous seem pompous. It's the British way.

Later, the famous runner Eric Liddell comes to town, makes a speech, then runs. Apparently, he's a rock star of running, even though it's the time of Jazz. He's the apple of Scotland's eye. Children beg for his autograph. There wasn't much to cheer about in Scotland in the 1920s. There's more tweed in this film than in most films and it looks as if the temperature rarely rises above gloomy. There doesn't seem to be a color shown on screen that is not grey or beige.

There is a big push for the proper representation of Christianity, which I didn't realize was in such dire straits at the time, to be represented by Eric Liddell and his fame. Terms like 'Running in God's name' and Jesus are banded about. His wife is in a perpetual state of anxiety. Maybe he's a philanderer, or maybe she's concerned about his running style, which is similar to a toddler stumbling down a steep incline. It's clear there's going to be a conflict of interests in Liddell's pursuits of greatness through God and Jesus, and the rising star of Harold Abrahams, a Jew, who is just trying to prove his equality.

It's obvious Eric Liddell is a superior talent among his competitors, but it's also very obvious this film is not about the four-minute mile. That is confirmed when I do some research and realize nothing about the film involves the four-minute mile *at all*. The first person to run the four-minute mile was Sir Roger Bannister, an Englishman who achieved that goal in 1954... 30 years after the 1924 Olympics which becomes the focus of *Chariots's* later drama. Obviously, I got my famous British runners confused. My two years of research between my initial inspirational daydream and my first training session to break the four-minute mile were sincerely wasted.

Still, I continue. Abrahams and Liddell go head-to-head in a 100-yard dash and Liddell smokes him. Abrahams is in awe and soon becomes obsessed in his quest to be as good, and *better* than Liddell. Abrahams hires Sam Mussabini as his coach, who has trained many Olympic champs over the years. Sam is a cigar-chomping character right out of a movie, which is apt because this is a movie.

Eventually, the film gives me what I want and need. What everyone wants and needs... a montage of training sequences where both Abrahams and Liddell get better. It's no *Rocky IV* montage sequence... in fact all 37 *Rocky* films have better training sequences, but this is still good. They run with dogs, run with motorcycles, run with sweaters, and run on the wet surf. Apparently, having soggy shoes is something these people enjoy.

Considering these athletes are training to run, they do an awful lot of drinking and smoking. Lord Andrew Lindsay, a filthy rich fellow student and competitor to Abrahams, having smoked a cigarette, jumps over hurdles, each topped with champagne glasses filled to the brim with bubbly. I assume once he completes the task successfully without knocking them over, he'll drink them all up.

Because this film is not about the four-minute mile at all, my attention began to wane... but here's the last hour rundown...

Drama; British things; powerful people suggesting

Abrahams lose because it will shadow the Christianity thing; anger; resentment; blah blah blah… then, finally, some actual color enter the beige film… red, white, and blue. The Americans! Then, other countries! Flags of the world… Then, some REAL color…a black man – at least I think I see one… something most of these pale people haven't seen. I'm not sure he even competes. Were black people allowed to compete? I doubt it. Sign of the times.

Continuing…

Olympics, etc; drama; montages; Vangelis music; the main guy from the film *Breaking Away*, a film about bicycle riding and not running; running heats; eliminated competition; slow motion running, handshakes, cheering and smiling; a shit-load of straw boater hats; Abrahams gold medal; champagne; mixed emotions; Liddell win; God; gold; Vangelis music; all is forgiven because sometimes British gold medals are more important than God; Finally, acceptance; love; Funeral; running on the beach to Vangelis Oscar-winning theme song; Credits.

Did I find inspiration in this film? Yes. Is it better than *Raiders of the Lost Ark*? Absolutely not. Is it better than *Rocky IV*? Not really. Did the film serve the purpose I set out to find which was inspiration to run the four-minute mile? That remains to be seen.

Raiders absolutely deserved the Oscar for best film, that is very clear. One film is about a guy punching Nazis, a deplorable group who are very anti-Jew, and one film is about a Jew trying to show his worth in the world he may not necessarily fit into. Perhaps they could combine the two concepts and make a movie about the Olympics, running and defeating the Nazis... an action-packed adventure about Jesse Owens, an American black man who won four gold medals in Berlin against Hitler's Aryan competitors. That is a film guaranteed to win multiple gold medals at the Academy Awards.

4

One of my biggest regrets was not playing basketball at a high level as a youth.

Like many delusional males long past their prime dates, I was convinced I could have been a contender. This regret/realization came when I was around 29 years-old and found myself playing pickup hoops on the courts of Manhattan. I'd arrive to a cluster of courts at the Houston Playground on the corner of Houston and Chrystie Streets in the Bowery. I'd mingle with the eclectic cast – all of them ready to play serious blacktop hoops. It was a meeting of various worlds… an amalgamation of neighborhood teens, broken-down ex-college players, thugs, enthusiastic Chinese from nearby Chinatown, and the occasional delusional white guy from the 'burbs. No one really said much, one simply wandered onto the court, and when there was 5 on 5, we just started playing.

Eventually, I hooked up with a guy named Chris, an ex-Uconn Husky, or perhaps he was a Villanova Wild Cat (I can't remember, some kind of snow animal) who blew out his back in college and couldn't jump high enough to slide a sheet of paper under his feet. But Chris had incredible court vision and a stellar basketball IQ. With his court vision and my athleticism, we began running an unstoppable pick and roll game that decimated unsuspecting victims thinking we were two guys who just met at a pick-up game. His Stockton to my Malone. Except he was black, and I was white.

Then, on a sunny summer day, the realization came that I potentially missed my calling as a high draft pick in the NBA lottery. Don't laugh.

At the top of the three-point line, I passed Chris the ball at the left elbow and cut to the basket. He dished me a sky-high alley-oop pass that I had to go up higher than expected to grab, which I wrangled and slam-dunked, my first ever flush. I came down from my lofty heights, knees buckling and crashed into the chain-link fence to the sounds of whoops and hollers. Not only was it a pretty slam, but it was the game winner. I was met with high-fives and murmurs as I met each hand with a slap and crooked grin – surprised at myself. That's when I realized that I should have pursued the game… an epiphany 20 years too late.

Weeks later in another game where Chris and I were on opposing teams, I had the ball on the left post and Chris was my defender. I went up with a fake, which Chris bit on by jumping more than a paper sliver high. I rolled past him towards the basket and he karate-chopped me across the arms, sending the ball flying out of bounds. It was a good foul. Unfortunately, he blew out his back again. He placed his palm on the base of his spine and gingerly walked off the court and down the street. It was the last time I ever saw him. He never called me, and I never dunked the ball again.

This is where I peaked in the realm of personal athletic achievement. It was all downhill from there. My star had risen and quickly fell. After a solid year on the courts, I stopped playing. I then dedicated myself to the personal achievements of pushing my liver and lungs to the edge of endurance with toxins in both liquid and smoke form.

Getting to the NBA is about as unrealistic a dream as one could pray for. It's a one in a million shot. It's like movie star or rock musician. Very difficult to achieve. It takes hard work, dedication, some luck, and occasionally, it requires a few connections.

Just about every kid has a dream of becoming a famous athlete, someone world-renowned in their sport and adored by fans in their pursuit of a championship. I was an excellent football player and excelled in pee wee football as a quarterback, but as I got older, my weight stayed the same and everyone else rose. A 5' 9" 120-pound 12-year-old is as common as a tree, but a 6 foot, 140 pound 18 year-old is not. I watched as everyone around me got thicker and I stayed relatively the same. I played lacrosse for a few weeks before a rival mid-fielder shattered my wrist with a tomahawk chop across the arm with his stick, and the following year I missed my career as a volleyball player when I tangled legs with the guy across the net going for a spike, fell back, and cracked my other wrist bracing myself against the floor.

Still, even the best of the best of my classmates were no match for the professional athletes. The cream of the crop. If you've ever been around an NBA basketball player or an

NFL middle linebacker, you'll know what I mean. These people are MASSIVE. They are the physical Gods of the earth. Flawed as they are in their personalities, their morals, and their life choices, no one can deny they aren't awe-inspiring physical specimens in person. Watching a 7-foot, 275-pound human lower their head through a doorway as they enter a room is like watching a giraffe poke his head through the window to say hello. It's absolutely shocking. My father once met Lawrence Taylor, the legendary New York Giants linebacker at a charity event and was dumbfounded by his size… and my father is not a small man. He talked about it for a week.

With that said, there's certainly a spot in the athletic Pantheon for those who don't mow-down quarterbacks after plowing through a line of men pushing 400 pounds. None of those behemoths can run a four-minute mile, no doubt, but they can't do a lot of activities – like run marathons, ride a bicycle 2,235 miles, nor flip around on the gymnasium uneven bars. There's a sport for every one of every size. Truly. Ask any person riding a horse in the Kentucky derby.

Unfortunately, there's a small window to accomplish these athletic dreams and it helps to have these dream far earlier in your life. Trying to draw the eyes of NBA scouts at 25 means you missed your mark by *at least* 5 years. The body doesn't get too much stronger after 30, and your ability to land a punch, get mauled by large men, or land squarely on your feet from a height higher than a few feet, drops considerably.

In fact, just about every athlete that has excelled in their field is put out to pasture by 35 and a few rare birds have made it to 40… and the ones that do extend beyond that age tend to be freaks of nature, even in regards to the 1% category they already inhabit. Depending on the extent of stress put on the body, some have even pushed 50, but it's not someone in the business of full contact sports.

My dream of running a four-minute mile is fantasy at best. I took a walk around the neighborhood with my wife and son on a freezing winter day and besides the pains of their insistent whining about the cold, was the random pains I felt in my body along the way.

At one point my wife asked me a question, which I couldn't hear because my hearing isn't what it used to be (let's not get into *that* subject), and when I turned to hear what she repeated, a shooting pain shot through my hip like I'd been spiked with a spear. I bit my lip and bared it, but if I can't turn 45 degrees to listen to a question; how can I expect to run a four-minute mile? I suppose when running the four minutes, there'll be very little turning other than the very slight turn of the oval track, so I'll be running more or less in a straight line. I won't need to turn my head or twist myself at all. Just full speed ahead. The way I like it. But the hip pain was concerning.

Side note: Much like the slight turn of the track, my hearing has been disappearing to the point that I barely noticed until one day I asked my family to turn up the TV and they responded "really?" and clicked the volume button. I watched the volume numbers on the TV go from 28 up to 35, which, regardless of your TVs volume control setting, means you've gone WAY past the point of absurdity. If you have your own separate house, it's fine, but anyone living in an apartment or in close quarters means you'll be getting a knock on the door.

Signs like the hip pain could mean I may have peaked even in the simple task of running a straight line. Hearing loss, knee pain, complete and utter contempt for anything other than sitting around watching TV are tell-tale signs you should enjoy sports vicariously through others.

At one point in my life, I wanted to play in a Super Bowl. Now I'm discomforted by the activity of eating my vegetarian chili I make every Super Bowl if the Chili is too hot – and I mean hot as in temperature, but I also mean spicy as well! If the chili is too spicy, I can't sleep at night. Rest is essential for old folks. A bad night's sleep is the equivalent of being hungover. Bad sleep can disrupt your weekly workout schedule, which means in the pursuit of athletic goals like the four-minute mile, you have to "restart" the quest. Statements like, "I'm going to start doing this FOR REAL next week" pop into the head. Wrapped up in warm blankets on cool mornings when I should be leaping from the bed on my way to the gym are replaced with slow sips of coffee and the statement, "I'll start tomorrow." That type of sloth will get me nowhere fast.

There must be some level of dedication. Some discipline. No more statements like: "Just one more drink and I'll call it a night." The drinks rarely stop and before you know it, you're calling an Uber to drive your drunk ass to your car a block away. No more, "I'll eliminate the red meat this week" as you're biting into a steak. There's no one to convince but yourself. There's no one to crack the whip but the man in the mirror; so, if there's a goal to meet, it must be met behind the guidance of the nose on your face.

I once read about a woman whose stomach was fermenting her own alcohol, causing her to be in a perpetual state of drunkenness.

Isn't that wonderful?

Unfortunately, she was blowing high blood alcohol levels on breathalyzer tests and her employers were tossing her in the streets thinking she was a lousy drunk. Although some people would kill for this type of physical malformity, it's the ones that are formed through hard work, sweat, and determination that are most gratifying.

My dedicated regiments on the treadmill were in danger of washing away with apathy, laziness and a heaping dose of aches and pains.

To remain steadfast in my pursuit of this dream, I needed to do everything I felt I needed to do, regardless of all the roadblocks that appear in the road... eliminate the heavy Chinese food dinners; the crispy cold beers the night before; and toss aside that damn Ugg comforter my wife bought that weighs somewhere in the range of 15 pounds and feels like a sheet of leaded cotton balls that push me against the mattress like some kind of suffocating gravity. Will power is what's needed over all other factors and to have that means training the brain. That means getting serious... getting focused... getting REAL.

Besides the will to do it and the focus to maintain a course, I needed the proper training materials. Clothing.

5

In the 1980s, every time I saw someone running, I mean someone *really* dedicated to the act of running, they were wearing tiny little shorts that fluttered on the sides like wings. These tiny shorts, cut three millimeters below the crotch, and made of a material lighter than oxygen, would rise towards the hip in a V and left little to the imagination for someone observing them running. Especially the men.

From 1950 to about 1985, professional basketball players wore shorts so short, their testicles practically hung from the gap in the leg. Watching old footage of Kareem Abdul Jabbar or Wilt Chamberlain, both with legs longer than California Redwood trees, standing at mid court, hands on their hips, huffing for oxygen in basketball shorts no longer than a child's swimsuit, gives off strong vibes of second-hand embarrassment. It wasn't until Michael Jordan began wearing mid-thigh shorts in 1986 when things began to change. It was the shot heard round the world... and I don't mean a basketball shot.

Athletes far and wide asked, "I don't need to wear shorts where my man parts may poke out after an aggressive jump?" And the world said "NO, you don't." Somewhere along the way it went to the extreme and players wore shorts cut to their ankles, but then it reverted back to the means. It will never rise to the ball sack again because I assume we've all decided there's a proper cut that is both tasteful and practical.

When I go to the gym, I wear whatever gym gear is laying over my computer chair that doesn't smell like a wildebeest. It consists of either my dark grey Nike shorts and a black T-Shirt, light green Nike shorts and a grey shirt donning a sports car that my afore-mentioned friend Stephen silk screened himself, or a pair of women's grey running shorts that I accidentally purchased at Dick's (ironically) that my dick can barely fit into and is eerily close to the 1980s basketball shorts Kareem may have donned in the NBA finals.

I'm not exactly a fashionista at the gym. Most men aren't. Most of the men at my gym look like they rolled out of bed and continued rolling until they entered the gym. They have bedhead, puffy eyes, mismatched socks and shorts with moth holes in them. The women pull themselves together a bit – wear fashionable, fitted clothing with seasonable colors. I obviously can't be bothered. I cork a ratty New York Jets hat on my head, toss on a sweatshirt I've had since I was 18 and go to the gym.

Researching men's running shorts I've found the style has improved, but not much. They're still high on the thigh, but sensible enough the scrotum won't be making an appearance for the world to see. The light material is the same and I assume there's no friction to slow down the process. At this stage of the game, anything could potentially slow me down. And I don't mean heavy steaks and red wine. Friction-causing shorts, loose shirts that catch the wind, and unsecured hair could add a precious second or two to the final time at the finish line. I must think about running style, technique, efficiency and clothing that cuts the wind.

There's something to be said about proper clothing and equipment, especially the shoes. Up until recently, I was wearing a pair of neon blue Nikes I bought on sale for $50 at the Shoe Warehouse. I got them in the discount section. Awesome deal. I wore them for 6 years and they were no longer neon blue. They were just *blue* blue. They were dirty from life, but the glow had diminished having used them not only at the gym, but for yard work and for painting the house. The blue blue became more evening blue, and the flecks of white paint that coated them gave the appearance of stars in the sky. My wife insisted I get new sneakers as these were considered "embarrassing." The same secondhand embarrassment I felt looking at Kareem Abdul Jabbar's nut sack was now being felt by my wife with my shoes. Going to the gym with a hobo was no longer an option for her, so I bought grey Nike sneakers that fit nicely, were stylish and were excellent for exercise. I know what you're thinking… "they make other colors of clothing." Yes, that's true. But I'm not in the factory dying these things. That's for small children living in impoverished countries to do. I'm here in America at the Nike store purchasing these things and the options are neon pink and candy blue, or grey. I chose grey. They're *athletic* sneakers; meaning they have no ties to any exercise genre. They can be used for running, baseball, javelin tossing and skeet shooting. They're made with a netting material that is breathable and turns my feet to ice at the slightest winter breeze.

My wife went to a running shoe store years ago and got a pair of Asics. The staff at the store had her run on a treadmill with computer analysis. Not one, but two people watched her run, examining her gate, foot placement and weight distribution. The computer spit out information on arch support, speed, and heal-to-toe-technique. When all was said and done, they gave her a pair of shoes that to *this day* she can't stop talking about as far as comfort and fit. Sort of like someone who talks about an amazing meal or a wonderful trip they took. I realize that good sneakers are essential; but how far do I need to go? My buddy Stephen referenced that book *Born to Run* about these people in Africa who ran barefoot on rocks and cactuses and shit, and were somehow *the greatest runners on earth*. I'm not sure whose handing out *that* award, but none of them had their feet analyzed by a computer. Yes, perfect shoes can be amazing, but I think the $125 Nikes I got that weren't tossed in the bargain bin, but on the actual shelf because they were decent, were good enough to attack the four-minute mile.

Going online to shop for sports clothing is to go down a rabbit hole of craziness. If you really want to attack it from every angle, you can. There's compression socks, slim-fit shirts, caps, ankle supporters and the list goes on. I figured a pair of white crew socks would be fine, but maybe I need to reconsider that. I don't know.

I constantly think back to the African people running with no shoes. Jim Thorpe, the great American (and Native American) Olympic athlete, won two gold medals wearing mismatched shoes he found in the trash. When he discovered someone had stolen his shoes during the 1912 Olympics, he fished two beat-up foot covers from a garbage pail and still somehow reached the top of the podium. Twice. I'm no Jim Thorpe, but there's got to be a point where the equipment can only do so much. The rest is up to me with the equipment I was born with – the heart, lungs, legs and all that stuff. Training those things to function at the highest level is up to the person wielding them.

I realize every second counts, but I don't intend to cross the finish line at the very last second, I intend to SHATTER the record with seconds to spare. I'll take into consideration wind, form, speed and equipment, but to cross the line in under four minutes will mostly be about the berserker energy I can exude during the process.

At this time, the only thing I can afford, both financially and timewise would be to tie my sneaker laces tighter instead of slipping my Nike's on like ratty house slippers. That's my first step (no pun intended) in performance enhancement.

6

On February 5th, after a night out with my family enjoying a rare restaurant meal, I come upon a dose of reality in the form of a Facebook post.

I'm informed that on "Saturday, February 1, Ethan Strand Obliterates the Collegiate Indoor Mile Record, who ran 3:48.32, the third-fastest time ever for the indoor mile. Strand is now Number 3 on the all-time list in the event. Only Ethiopia's Yomif Kejelcha (3:47.01 in 2019) and American Yared Nuguse (3:47.38 in 2023) have ever run faster indoors."

This is a sobering punch in the face. One reason is the picture of Stand, who looks like I did at his age, appears to be in *way* better shape than me. The news that 11 1/2 seconds is "shattering a record" is also very sobering.

Yet, serendipitously, this is the motivation I've been searching for to tackle my task. Not *Rocky IV*, not *Chariots of Fire*, and certainly not any Hollywood production. It's good old-fashioned bulletin board material. Strand is now *my* muse.

My Michael Jordan. My Eric Liddell. My Stephen Spielberg.

Although enthusiastic, my week gets rough. Thursday, I run for 18 minutes at a casual pace, then hit the weights. I didn't even regard the running distance. I just wanted to get my heart and lungs in better shape. I ran half that time on the elliptical machine, which if you are unfamiliar the quirky device, is one of those stepping machines that forces you to ungulate in circles unnaturally, like someone running on a lake with 5-gallon water cooler bottles as shoes. It helps with impact – good for geezer knees… and hips, and ankles, and feet. The rough part comes when I go to bed enthusiastic for a fresh Friday of training and awaken feeling like something dredged from a lake. I go to the gym but do only 10 minutes of random crap before I call it quits.

I was back on track (no pun intended) a few days after Super Bowl Sunday, where I needed recovery time from my small hangover. Then I was delayed from getting to the gym due not to one, but *two* severe snowstorms.

Ok, in all transparency, one of those storms dropped three inches, and the second storm dropped what looked like something coated atop of a funnel cake. The first storm did require I go out and shovel, so I got a decent amount of exercise for that one. But the second simply kept me in bed because I was super cozy, and my wife was warm and toasty next to me. I know, not exactly the internal fortitude of a champion runner. But a few days later I was on the treadmill and had my best time. 12:53. I think the snow shoveling really helped my cardio. Still, I was laboring in the breathing. If my training sequence was in a film, it would be called *Chests of Fire*, because I felt a burning in my entire solar plexus like I swallowed a hot coal.

I know what you're thinking... "Don't you think about anything else but films?" and I reply to that question with my own question: "Didn't we already have this conversation?" The answers are yes, I do, and yes we did... and... I also think about music too.

To keep my motivation in peak condition, I put together a playlist of songs to inspire me... to push me over the top when I feel myself fading. Speaking of over the top, Stallone was in an arm-wrestling movie called *Over The Top* and although a pretty stupid movie, it does.... Ok, you know what? Let's focus on music.

Here's my playlist, mostly songs about running, or with running in the title.

Running down a Dream – Tom Petty
(What can I say? It is the embodiment of what I'm trying to achieve. Running and running down a dream, both physically and metaphorically. About as catchy and inspirational a running tune as one could listen to.)

Born to Run – Bruce Springsteen
(Another classic. Even though I've heard this song 5,000,000 times in my life, it means a little bit more while running)

When The World Is Running Down, You Make the Best of What's Still Around – The Police
(A low-key classic off one of my favorite albums Zenyatta Mondatta. Fantastic running song. Good beat.)

Running on Empty – Jackson Browne
(I like to think I'm running on full, but a good running song. It's also part of that *Forrest Gump* running montage where he runs across country. As I've stated, I enjoy movies, montages, and movies with montages.)

Run to the Hills – Iron Maiden
(Fun song to run to, yet I'm running towards more level ground, similar to the level ground a four-minute mile runner would want to run on.)

Running Up That Hill – Kate Bush
(Good tune, but again, no hills. I'm not running to them, nor up them.)

Run Like Hell – Pink Floyd
(Is there any other way to run?)

Running with the Devil – Van Halen
(There's a Hell theme running here... see what I did there?)

Run to You – Bryan Adams
(Great running song – I like to think Bryan is singing about the finish line.)

I Ran – Flock of Seagulls
(although this should be listened to *after* a run, I enjoy it while running.)

Running with the Night – Lionel Richie
(Another fantastic running song and very 1980s – synth, funky baseline, and of course, Lionel Richie.)

Run Through the Jungle – Credence Clearwater Revival
(Nice CCR rocker. Much like the Hill thing that was referenced earlier, there's no jungle to run through. Just track.)

Running on a Treadmill – Oingo Boingo
(another song that embodies running, especially on a treadmill, but it's also a little goofy.)

Songs I rejected:

Take the Money and Run – Steve Miller Band
(this is a non-paying gig and not a good beat to run to.)

The Long Run – Eagles
(Way too slow. This is a song to listen to while sitting on pillows, drinking sweet wine and nibbling on cheap cheese.)

Running to Stand Still – U2
(Even slower. I love U2, but this is a song for staring out the window on rainy days.)

Run for your Life – The Beatles
(I love The Beatles even more than U2 but this is too much of a folky jaunt. Time signature is more of a stomp.)

Band on the Run – Paul McCartney and Wings
(Paul McCartney's attempt to recreate side two of Abbey Road has too many time signatures to be a consistently good running song.)

Runner's High – The Hold Steady
(Generic rock bullshit, I don't think the phrase 'Runner's High' is mentioned once.)

Take it on the Run – REO Speedwagon
(Not a big Speedwagon fan, but this almost made it. It's slightly too slow. Maybe for jogging, but not an all-out run. Besides, what is REO taking on the run? The song makes no sense.)

Grandma Got Run Over by a Reindeer – the Christmas Folks
(Do I really need to say more?)

Run-Around – Blues Traveler
(Too jaunty. This is for children and potheads to spin around in circles at a small bar with a pool table and jukebox.)

It Keeps You Running – Doobie Brothers
(Great song. Good Michael McDonald warbler, but not exactly an energy booster. Maybe for a light jog, but not running.)

Besides my well curated playlist to inspire my running, I was inspired by the music of my son Max (trombone) at his high school band's mid-season performance where they played such classics as *Critical Mass* by Todd Slater and

Among the Clouds by Brian Balmages. A fine night out getting culture with classical music.

7

The next morning, after a solid night's sleep, some stored carbs from a two slice cheese pizza dinner from the night before (even though I have gluten issues), and a greenish banana for breakfast, I stormed out of the gate and "shattered" my previous treadmill time by crushing a 10:29. Almost a full two and a half minutes better than my 12:53 the day before.

Even though the bottom of my left foot stiffened up at the beginning, I pushed through. Not only that, I also felt good immediately afterwards and the hours that proceeded it. For the first time since starting this adventure, I felt as if my (day) dream wasn't so far out of reach. Yes, I still need to shave a full six and a half minutes off my time and yes, *chests of fire* and all that, but I could see reality beginning to take shape. With a little more dieting, some more training, and a little (see: a lot) less drinking, I could hit a new 'best' time, which will slingshot me into a new bout of inspiration, which will parlay into another bout of inspiration, and then another, and another.

And although I fully intended to break the four-minute mile mark, I decided, out of curiosity, to search online: "What is the fastest time a 53-year-old man has run the four-minute mile?"

That answer, according to Google, was achieved by a man named Brad Barton, who ran the "four-minute mile" in 4:19.59 in the 50-54 Age Group.

This was inspiring in two ways:

One, I had no idea there were age group brackets, so I knew I could find a niche to snuggle into somehow as a conciliatory prize.

Two, I now had another muse to look up to – Brad Barton. Sounds like the name of a bully you'd see in one of those bad teen movies who flicks people's ears or bestows atomic wedgies until he eventually gets his comeuppance by the unlikely hero who humiliates him by tossing him into a vat of cow dung or something like that. I know... more movie references. I'm sure Brad Barton is a nice guy. I have no idea, but I assume so. He's now Muse 2.0.

Another factoid I found on my Goggle dive was an average four-minute running time chart for men and their age brackets on Marathon Sports:

AgeGroup	Beginner	Novice	Intermediate	Competitive	Elite
20-30	9:25	7:48	6:37	5:46	5:08
30-40	9:39	8:00	6:47	5:54	5:16
40-50	10:18	8:32	7:14	6:19	5:37
50-60	11:08	9:14	7:50	6:49	6:05
60-70	12:09	10:04	8:32	7:26	6:38

Then, I found some training tips to improve running on the same website. Tips about schedule, strength training, nutrition and hydration, and a bunch of other stuff I'll probably ignore, but probably shouldn't.

Then on the website for the Harvard Review, there was a good article about the history of the four-minute mile and Roger Bannister by Bill Taylor. In this article, he describes Roger Bannister as the rebel of running at that time. He didn't have a formal trainer and ran by his own methods outside the running world's eye.

I felt a kinship with him immediately.

I said, "yeah, I'm a rebel too! I have discount sneakers and woman's shorts and ripped t-shirts from friends. I don't care!"

What was most interesting about this article was the fact that 46 days after Roger Bannister broke the four-minute mile, it was accomplished again by Australian John Landy. It seems Bannister broke the seal, so to speak. Showing the world the four-minute mile was breakable, others began to accomplish the goal knowing it could finally be done. In fact, just a year later, three runners broke the four-minute mile in a single race. With actual proof of accomplishment, the goal was met many times over the decades that followed. 1,800 times.

Then… I get home from work that very evening to see a video on social media. Less than a few weeks after Ethan Strand broke the indoor NCAA four-minute mile world record, Norwegian runner Jakob Ingebrigtsen broke the indoor four-minute mile world record set in 2019 by Yomif Kejelcha (3:47.01) with the stunning time of 3:45.15 at the 117th Millrose Games, which took place at the Armory in New York City.

What I failed to see during the time I was compiling my completely ridiculous music playlist was that four days prior to *that* record-breaking run by Ingebrigtsen, Kejelcha's record had already been broken by Yared Nuguse (3:46.63) who did it at the same 117th Millrose Games!

In the month of February 2025 alone, *three* world records had been broken... one broken just days after it'd been set. It's truly a stunning set of circumstances. In fact, watching the race where Ingebrigtsen breaks the record, every single runner in the race breaks the four-minute mile. Some of them with ease! I'm not sure if I should give up or carry on knowing it can be done by so many at such a break-neck pace.

A few days later, Grant Fisher breaks the 5,000-meter record. It's not the four-minute mile, but it's a string of world records that are dropping at an unprecedented rate. I feel inspired, but I'm nervous some other old fart will swoop in and break the four-minute mile record before me, forcing me to push myself to a place I'm not sure I can go... or I fear at the very least, someone may break the fastest time in my age group.

Looking at these runners, they're thin, fit and are competing at a high level. They're wearing ball-hugging onesies and definitely feeding on grape seed oil and high protein yogurts. My only advantage I believe at this point in time, is having less wear-and-tear on my legs. My fresh knees could give me the edge over those who may try and break the record in my age group. Those runners, usually running lifers, have probably worn their legs to the bone with the excessive pounding of their feet in the streets.

I had to refocus and double my efforts.

8

One of my best sports as a kid, although I never pursued it competitively at a high level, was swimming.

Swimming, whether in the ocean or in a pool, is one of the few sports where you can actually die doing it. You could die in the decathlon if you walked onto the field and was struck in the head by a discuss or spiked in the sternum with a javelin. Even a golf ball to the skull could cause a brain contusion. But with swimming, drowning is a very real thing. Fortunately, I'm a strong swimmer.

My grandparents had a pool, and I swam for years. I could swim underwater holding my breath going from one side of the pool to the other, without coming up for air. It's where I learned about oxygen in the blood and lung space. Before diving in, I would breathe deeply multiple times – essentially hyperventilating to the point of passing out – then dive in and accomplish my goal. Sometimes I'd exceed two laps and get another half pool length before exploding to the surface in a bout of dramatic inhalation.

This breathing technique was taught to me by my father, who swam a lot as a kid too. As a teen, he was a lifeguard at community pools and local beaches. Running out to rough water and hauling a limp person back to shore requires an incredible amount of strength. Even if it's never performed in real life, you must do it to pass the lifeguard test. Oxygenating the blood is required to do the job well. Long, deep breaths, pulled into the chest through the diaphragm is the only way to endure intense exercise.

This blood oxygenation became more and more apparent as an essential technique the more I went through the process of training for this run. Not only oxygenation before the run, but while running itself. The body must be an oxygen machine. Not only does the body need strong, efficient running form, but it must be fit enough to intake and exhale breath at a machine-like rate. For many people, including myself, it feels natural to hold the breath while exerting tremendous force. Many people inhale and hold while pushing heavy weight… bench presses, arm curls, squats, etc. It feels good to hold and push. But it's not the correct technique.

I've heard certain trainers recommend breath IN during the exertion part of the workout. That is a philosophy I whole-heartedly disagree with. Who is going to squat 300 pounds while breathing in? It's insanity. Holding breath while exerting force, or pushing massive amounts of weight can take you over the top – a one second deadlift, or a snatch-and-grab over the head can certainly bear the pressure of a held breath without causing the heart to explode. But running a four-minute mile requires a constant, almost *obsessive* intake and outtake of breath.

Running at the rate of 15 miles an hour borders on dangerous for most humans not trained to do so. The body must become and cardiovascular machine, oxygenating the blood at a rate that's almost impossible to maintain because the body loses more oxygen than it can replace. If a human could somehow push further than four minutes running 15 miles per hour, say five minutes at 15 miles per hour, the rate could potentially kill them.

The only way to replicate that kind of speed vs. time would be if the person was literally running for their life, escaping a torturous prison, running from the police, or running to save a loved one from death. That type of adrenaline is impossible to replicate without an injection. And one never knows when a life and death situations will come about. Usually not before a structured race with other runners at the starting line. So, one must train the body like one is running for their life and able to replicate that type of scenario in the training.

I don't know what drugs or techniques are being used in the running games where these recent records are dropping like flies. Are they breathing with oxygen tanks? I know some cyclists have been known to inject their own stored oxygenated blood before the Tour De France. I'm not that dedicated. I mean, *I am* dedicated, but the thought of a needle entering my body to inject oxygenated blood before a run makes my skin crawl. Sounds like a dystopian nightmare of the future. An athlete shouldn't feel like their armor is compromised by an external sword, even if it is for the betterment of the performance. The body should feel whole, without holes, to perform at the highest level.

International boxing legend Manny Paquiao, who I watched grow from a scrawny kid to a fireplug of a man, refused to be tested for performance enhancing drugs before a match. He felt needles in the skin would compromise his body, and I agree with him. Of course, it immediately raised the red flags of performance enhancing drugs. How could it not? Any athlete refusing blood testing at the highest level before a huge match, especially one where the purse was worth millions, if not TENS of millions of dollars, is suspect. The media will inflate that speculation to maximum levels. I assume every athlete in every sport is taking something to enhance their performance. Steroids, HGH... God knows what else. 300-pound men don't usually run a 40-yard dash in 5 seconds. Yet somehow these American football players accomplish the goal often. Who am I to judge?

I'm not sure how performance enhancing drugs could elevate a four-minute mile runner. Perhaps I'm naive. I know steroids can help a man lift more weight, can make a football player bigger, stronger and faster... but can it truly help them run a mile in under four minutes?

That accomplishment feels like a battle of the wills.

A goal that is met with the mind.

A goal that is accomplished when the brain tells the body that together, they are going to accomplish this dream.

Yes, it will be difficult... perhaps almost impossible, but if the brain is not on board; can the body truly be? And once the brain is on board, the body must be as well. Can the brain be completely aboard the journey and not the body? I suppose so. If the body does not, or cannot be fit enough to accomplish the goal, then yes, it most certainly cannot be part of the goal. But sometimes the brain must tell, or even *trick* the body to do more than it thinks it can.

People can always be pushed further than they believe they can, but that is usually by an outside force. The person who is pursuing a goal such as the four-minute mile, especially me doing it outside any establishment, must be the force, the will, the motivation, and the executioner of the task and goal. I must become obsessive to a level beyond what anyone can be a part of because to achieve the goal is a reward for no one but the person crossing the finish line – myself. And no amount of external motivation can push anyone more than that.

The great athletes of the world, the Jordans and Muhammed Alis became themselves through a force that can't be replicated by anyone but them, the person pumping the blood in that particular heart.

My will to achieve this goal must outweigh the will of other things in my life. The fear of failure, the tempestuous call of food and wine, and the doubt in the mind of the physical accomplishment itself.

But I must also trim myself in ways I ignored before the idea entered my head. I must treat my body as a machine, give it excellent fuel, train every part of the body for maximum performance, because everything is attached and must work in unison. I must get my calves, thighs, hips and core muscles tight and strong. They must be coordinated in the function. I must practice efficient technique, with legs running at proper pace, core tight, but loose enough to inhale breath deeply and to maximum capacity. My arms must be tight to the body and swing effortlessly and not be a detriment to overall effica-ciousness. Even my hair, which used to be chopped short and is now long, must be gelled back and sculpted to the skull so it can buffer the wind and not cause friction or be a distraction. It must be smooth like the cyclist's helmet... slick like the fish that slips through the stream. I must slice the wind – cut the air like a knife.

I must also contemplate my timing and speed. Do I run as fast as possible at the beginning and use what's left in my tank to stubble to the end? Do I try and pace myself even-ly throughout the run? Should my gate be that of a gazelle, whose long strides can cover a large amount of space? Or should I strive for cleaner, even leaps that are less strenuous on the hips and knees and stretch the hamstrings like rubber bands?

The answers come in the doing, and so I will do. I don't intend to use any performance enhancing drugs because not only are my drug days over, but I wouldn't know where to get them if I wanted. I don't know pushers. I don't know weightlifters or superior athletes. I'm very resourceful and I'm sure I could hunt these things if necessary, but I won't.

They say drug addicts have a work ethic higher than most to obtain their high, or to prevent drug sickness, but I'm not an addict. I'm just a guy who wants to run, so I will do what I can within my control and do it well. I will eat, drink and train with running in my mind... with running in my heart. I will make it my drug and my obsession... and accomplish my goal the old-fashioned way – with stubborn, obsessive, razor-sharp focus.

9

Because this is a book and not a movie, I will describe my training sessions in literal montage detail. Close your eyes and picture it... wait, don't close your eyes. You need to read this. Open your mind's eye and see this...

Montage begins:

At work, A.J. stares at his phone and shakes his head
The phone plays a video of Ingebrigtsen beating the four-minute mile.

A.J. spins in his office chair, stares into the distance, stands, goes to the window and looks down into the parking lot below where the people resemble ants. He's both inspired and touched with a twinge of fear in his heart.

Cut to:

A.J. at the dinner table. He's eaten two cheeseburgers (sirloin) and fries, while sipping a large glass of red wine. He's stuffed. He shakes his head knowing he's eaten too much.

Dissolve to:

Later, he eats ice cream on the couch while watching a terrible rom com about a guy and his daughter who buy a villa in Italy. He shakes his head (again) at the bad acting, the obvious direction the film is taking, and the ice cream, which has been too heavy and unhealthy.

Cut to:

The next morning, while sipping coffee on the couch, A.J. looks out the window where the cold rain falls in sheets. He's inspired to go to the gym. He nods enthusiastically, like that meme of a heavily bearded Robert Redford from the film *Jeremiah Johnson*.

      "I wanna go to the gym," he says to his wife, Rita.
      "You wanna go?" she asks.
      He nods.
      "I want to run... fast!" he says.
      "Okay," she says, "let's go."
      They leap from the couch.

End montage.

We get to the gym and of course the place is mobbed. Everyone has the same idea... *go to the gym on this cold, rainy day.* There's not one treadmill available. I stretch and prepare my body for a run. After that, there's still no treadmills.

So, I wait. I become annoyed.

A man hops off and I hop on, but he returns to let me know that he was still using it and only went to the desk to hand them a lost phone. I'm annoyed, but the man did a kind thing.

I wait again.

Eventually a limping, heavy older man who looks as if he can barely walk, steps off a treadmill and I hop on. He comes and cleans it for me… I appreciate it.

Then, I go at it.

Right out of the starting gate, I hit 7 miles per hour and gallop a clean eighth of a mile then go to 8 miles per hour. I go another full loop, drop to 7mph, then back to 8mph and continue and do another. I can't remember any time, but I eventually drop to 4 miles per-hour for a bit and rest. I'm breathing well, like a machine, but the stamina is not great. After a few seconds, I'm back to 7mph, then 8 mph. Even though I'm pushing myself harder than ever and my lungs are huffing like they haven't huffed in years, I cross with my best time.

9:07

Just like that, I'm in the triple digits.

Although enthusiastic and exhausted, I know there will be instances on this road where I'll take "a few steps forward and a step back." That's just life in pursuit of a goal. I've already prepared myself mentally for the inevitable day when I come into the gym and simply cannot best my time. It may not be now, or the next week, but it will come. And when the time does come, I'll be prepared.

I do a fast walk for another lap, then end my run by doing a 9mph dash for about 20 seconds before the tank is completely empty.

Afterwards, I cough a bit and release some light phlegm. I suppose having reached down into the lesser used parts of the lungs has dredged up some stuff. Sort of like the bottom of the ocean. The sludgy things we don't see on the seabed that get churned up during a bad storm, or an aggressive boat passing, or by unknown currents. Things like Fish bones, black mud and a guy with concrete shoes.

If you're like my wife, you don't like snot and phlegm talk, but that's just the ways of the human body – especially when it comes to training and physical activity. Running in cold weather produces snot, which must be expelled by spitting. Lungs not attuned to running a mile so fast will reactivate things that have been laying dormant.

I've never had asthma, but I do have allergy-induced breathing issues, and after this run, I feel tightening I haven't felt in a while. I go to a resource I haven't used in almost a year… the inhaler in my briefcase, which helps open my lungs immediately. Although the relief is minimal, it helps. I'm not sure how often I'll need to go to it for help, but for now, it's a necessary tool in the overall aspect of this adventure.

My wife and I go to the deli for lunch, which we bring home to eat with our son Max. I gobble down my ham and cheese omelet with a side of potatoes. I tell max about my goal and he's impressed. Especially someone *old and fat like me* – a continuing joke in our house. I'm old as dirt in comparison to him. Fat and old. If you looked at me, you'd see it was obvious sarcasm as I'm a 6-foot-tall man who having weighed himself at the gym that very day, came in at 179 pounds. It's heavier than I've been in a while, truth be told.

In all honesty, I'm bordering on "skinny-fat." If you are unfamiliar with that term, it means someone who seems to be fit, or at the very least, *thin*, yet when seen without their shirt, have a very discernible belly or soft middle. In some cases, it's extreme. The skinny person removes their shirt to expose a bulging gut that shocks those around them. I'm not that extreme physically, but I'm not exactly sporting a six-pack either. I'm soft in the middle. Like most 53-year-olds.

I have a "spare tire" around the lower midsection.

Not a car's spare tire.

That would indicate gluttony or irresponsibility.

More like a motorcycle spare tire… if motorcycles had spare tires.

Perhaps it's more of a lower-grade spare tire… say, a mountain bike tire… fatter than the thinner 'racing bicycle' tire used on the street, but more like the kind that goes on trails.

In relation to my wide shoulders, the spare tire is all balanced, but when isolating the belly with a narrow view, there's clearly work be done.

To help accomplish my goals, I must trim down, lose this chubby middle and get leaner. That will require disciple with the fork. I must eliminate almost entirely my gluten intake, which is not good for me anyway; my fat intake, which my doctor has been telling me to do for years; and I must uptake my vegetable intake, which I've been doing regardless because it makes me feel better.

It's been a long winter thus far and my body was inclined to pack on the pounds as a natural defense against the terrible New York winter weather. But at this juncture, it's time to get trim and fit. It was my plan regardless because I want to look good at the beach. Working out for years and displaying a belly makes all the gym time pointless if one cannot be fully happy once on full display. Now I have full reason to trim down. It's not about looks anymore. It's about hitting the goal. The mission. The dream.

Some experts, whoever they may be, will tell you to keep your dreams to yourself. Just put your head down and grind away. When you lift your head again, you may have accomplished your goal. You may also find the world passed you by. But the sentiment is sound. Walking around and crowing like a rooster about your big-time dreams is a recipe for failure. It's best to work behind the scenes and introduce yourself later as the success you are that nobody saw coming. That can be a lonely row to hoe.

I've learned through my writing that telling people what you're striving for serves up a decent amount of skepticism.

"Oh sure" … "Yeah right" and "Oh, really?" will ring in your head like buck shot.

So, I was skeptical about announcing to my wife and son, both who've heard my proclamations about 'someday' being a successful writer, that my new goal in life (aside from writing) was to REALLY beat the four-minute mile. I was elated to find they were supportive of this goal. I told them of Brad Barton, and the recent string of records broken at the Armory. Their support gave me a lift I didn't see coming. We talked immediately about training, quality food intake, and other thoughts regarding equipment, clothing and regiment.

My son, who ran track in school for a few years, told me his best time was six-something minutes. I don't think that's true because he has a terrible memory, but he told me that info after I told him most of the men beating the recent four-minute mile times look like him. Tall, lean men who run like greyhounds and slice the air because they're thin enough to cause little resistance. Max is not a man, but he's nearing six feet and he's athletic, with lean muscles and greyhound zip in his step. I was also at some of his track meets and I know for a fact he didn't run a six-something mile, but I'm sure his best had bested my best.

My new goal is to get to eight minutes and get to the halfway mark of my accomplishment. If I could do that in just a few weeks of starting this journey, that would be an accomplishment in and of itself.

10

I thought a good dinner of lean filet mignon, light mashed potatoes, and steamed broccoli... yes, and a little wine and ice cream, would be a reward for a job well done, but I awoke the next day after a restless night's sleep to a dizzy head and a very stiff left ankle.

During my time-breaking run the day before, I had one issue, and that was hydration. Even though I broke through, my mouth and throat became dry from the mechanical breathing. Waking in the morning practically hungover, I come to a very sobering conclusion... I must quit drinking alcohol. I'm not an alcoholic, but my weekly two to three nights of wine drinking must go down to zero, or as close to zero as possible, with only the rare special occasion when I drink just a bit. I must encompass the mind and body of an elite athlete if I'm to continue to break barriers and especially if I'm going to achieve the goal of oldest person to break the four-minute mile.

We all know the problems alcohol has on society, especially those with alcoholism or drinking problems. But even a mild drinker such as myself, who at one point was a heavy drinker, can have issues. The glass of wine after a terrible day, the pairing of a nice red wine with a steak, and the beer on Sunday with a game must be eliminated completely. Those cravings must be replaced with not only discipline, but focus. More training, more vision, more dedication and with healthy choices that don't include snacking, poor food replacements, and defaulting to old habits, some lingering since childhood. Habits like the urge to crunch chips, eat hunks of cheese from the fridge, or drink something sugary from a bottle.

Most doctors will probably tell you that drinking wine two or three nights a week is a lot, because if you add an extra day of drinking, you're then drinking more than half the week, and that is a lot. Alcohol takes its toll on the organs. The liver, kidneys, stomach – everything. Working to make the lungs high capacity while treating the other organs like a frat party is a blueprint for failure. I must hydrate, eat well and get lean. Even though I'm considered thin, I probably need to lose anywhere from 5 to 10 pounds. That weight will help with speed and take pressure of the knees. It's a mark of fitness and dedication and I must do it now.

Alcohol, besides being bad for the organs, is high in calories. A bottle of wine can average about 650 calories. Eliminating one and half to two bottles a week will eliminate 1,000 calories or more. Beer too. A can of beer can have anywhere from 150 to 200 calories. Those are empty calories and the alcohol itself dehydrates and robs the body of energy, stamina and overall health.

I hit the gym again in the early afternoon.

Having planned to see how close I could get to that eight-minute mark again, I readjust my plan and do a simple run. It's not a set-back but a smart idea. Keeping my body loose, the heart pumping and the blood flowing, while also giving myself proper rest, is the right idea. Attacking the four-minute mile every time I enter the gym is not the best idea. Having spent years at the computer, sedentary and sloth-like, then dashing into an aggressive attack of four-minute mile dreams could set me back in other ways. I must take smaller steps to build correctly. Rome wasn't built in a day, and four-minute miles weren't broken days after the decision to do so was made.

11

It was the Fall of 1982 and had just turned 11 years-old. I was *obsessed* with the game of football. I played it every chance I could. Even against our furniture, which needed to be replaced by the time I was 13. I was part of the PAL (Police Athletic League) on Long Island, one of the better organized sports leagues for youth sports. My team was The Hornets and we were the best team in the league, by far. I was the defensive cornerback and the backup quarterback and excelling at both. One night, after an intense Saturday evening game played in the rain, I was sitting on my bed, literally peeling the wet, muddy football pads off my cold, aching body with bloodied knuckles. I was facing the window, feeling like the 53-year-old man I am now after a football game. What I didn't realize was my mother had snuck into the room behind me and watched as I grimaced in pain after shedding each piece of equipment. She exploded in fear.

"That's it!" she shouted, "You're not playing this

game anymore!"

I spun around and exploded back.

"No, mom, no way! I love it. You can't make me stop!"

"You're in so much pain! I can't let you do this! You're going to get killed!"

I fell to my knees and grabbed at her hand.

"No. Ma! There's no way. I'm playing. You can't make me stop. Please!"

She shook her head… absolutely nonplussed. I could see the terror in her eyes. She'd seen the news. Heard the horror stories. Kids getting crippled. Young men moving like old men before they could have children themselves. She didn't want me to go on, and I didn't blame her. I was moving like a stiff, aching piece of wood. My knees creaked, my shoulders cracked, and I could barely lift my leg because of hip stiffness. That's not the kind of diagnosis you want from an 11-year-old athlete, but it comes with the territory. Especially with a contact sport like football.

"Ma, I'm fine." I told her. "I just need some ice."

She finally came around, but reluctantly.

"I'll get some ice."

Although this sounds like a terrible after-school special, it was not. This really happened. It's a memory seared into my brain. I'm going through it now with my son. The agony he feels after playing basketball. The ice on the sore knees after the hardwood pounding, the knots on the head from stray elbows... the bloody lips, the bruised thighs, the ripped flesh from fingernails of clawing, competitive hands. It's more than the thrill of victory and agony of defeat. It's the pain of intense competition. It's enough to make anyone hang it up and call it quits. One must endure to get over the top.

During my next run, the day after my time-breaking run, my calf muscle tightened up, causing mild pain, but not enough to make me stop. Most runners, especially those who run long distance such as the marathoner, tend to run a bit more flat-footed. It doesn't wear out the legs or rob the body of energy. To run fast, I need to spring from my step… launch off the foot to gain distance so the momentum stays in stride with the next step that comes down… especially if running at top speeds of 15 miles per hour. I've started running off the ball of my feet – using every muscle in the foot, ankle and calf to bounce off the ground. My legs are not used to that kind of employment.

Even when I did run for any length of time, it was without much discipline. Usually a flat-footed, smooth run with heavy doses of undulating upper body movements to co-ordinate with the hard blows of the feet against the ground. It's not ideal running. It's lazy running. It's the kind of running one does to "warm up" before hitting the weights. A simple five-to-10-minute run to get the blood pumping. That won't work for the four-minute mile. The kind of speed I need requires a body configuration I've not yet discovered but must understand. This spring-step technique may have contributed to my painful calf. As the night wore on, it became stiffer until it was difficult to walk.

I applied heat to the calf, and it helped loosen up the muscle, but of growing concern is the fact that I may have my first injury. These things happen to 53-year-olds, regardless of their prior shape and conditioning. It happens to 23-year-olds… and 13- year-olds. I must maintain a proper routine of stretching and when necessary, get the occasional massage.

Just as important as the task of running itself, is a proper deployment of weight training. It will strengthen muscles and prevent injuries. I already know from experience that low weight with high repetitions will get me longer, leaner muscles. The kind of muscles to help with speed. They're not the kind to show off at the beach if you desire body-builder results, but they look good regardless, and are excellent for speed and endurance.

Obviously, *all* the leg muscles are important in speed running, but my calves, which are in very good shape must get stronger, and my quads, which are also strong, must get stronger… but my area of immediate concentration is my hamstrings and more importantly, my Gluteus Maximus. The butt. The buns, bum, bootie, patootie, trunk, rump, tush, keister, rear, seat, tail, backside, behind, caboose. The posterior. The hindquarters. You know – the ass.

Because these muscles are behind me, as they are for most people, they're easy to ignore. Out of sight, out of mind.

As one of the great poets of our time, Sir Mix-A-Lot once stated… "You can do side bends or sit-ups, but please don't lose that butt."

As I've gotten older, my Gluteus Maximus has disappeared with lack of usage. This happens to a lot of men. Especially older white men. In the gym I'm able to get the haunches to return with squats and bridge thrusts, but it's a constant maintenance and it's clear I need to get the hams in tip top shape. Round. Strong. Powerful and fit. On the days I run less, I must develop these lacking areas more. I must evenly distribute the weight. Less in the middle and more down below.

12

A setback is ripe for a new beginning. At least that's how I'll frame it.

My calf strain has given me the opportunity to look at my training from a different perspective. I'm taking a lemon and turning it into a margarita. Even though margaritas are made with lime juice… and I quit drinking alcohol. But you get my point.

I'm approaching my training with a longer outlook, training to hit smaller goals instead of accomplishing the big goal in one intense shot. In celebration of my alcohol abstinence, I ate a large bowl of ice cream.

The next morning, I quit eating ice cream.

To celebrate quitting ice cream, I ate nothing. I must stop the urge to celebrate the simple things. If there's a constant celebration with a reward, the reward is usually a setback. So, my reward for accomplishing goals is pride in myself, and the thrill of the accomplishment.

Maybe smiling and nodding thinking about the accomplishment is the reward, as well as appreciating life.

My calf felt better but was still a bit tight. The day was bitterly cold, and the winds whipped at 40 mph. It was a good day to freeze *and* to freeze my training by eating light and resting. Also hydrating. My goal is to get my cardio-vascular system in the best shape it can be by running further and longer.

I will also completely adjust my eating habits. Besides losing weight, I must use the food as high-performance fuel to get my body performing at premium efficiency. I Googled "What do runners eat" to see what dietary restrictions those who run consume. I'm not sure why because I already knew the answer. Most likely brown rice, ancient grains, bland, unseasoned chicken breast, raw greens and other bland foods that are tasteless and are equated to sadness and boringness.

But after some reading, I see the choices are not too bad. I need carbs and good fats and lean proteins. Some highlights are eggs, peanut butter, salmon, beans, avocado and yogurt. Other things I need to consider is hydration, salt intake as well as a sports drink like Gatorade.

Other things needed for the body to perform at a high level whether it's running or not, is proper levels of vitamins. I take them occasionally but not frequently. I make sure iron levels are normal and I'm keeping my B vitamins in good supply. I eat enough to keep my vitamin levels normal, but with aggressive training, these things will have to be monitored.

It's man's inherent nature to torture himself, whether it's through the guilt of past indiscretions or by causing suffering through present trials. He can instill his self-wrath in any way he deems necessary by any way he chooses. If gluttony is the reward for a job well done, then starvation must certainly be the opposite spectrum for goals not yet met. To break the cycle of constant desserts, rich wines and steaks with a little too much fat, I've jumped into the deep end of the pool filled with roasted vegetable, lightly grilled chicken breast and everyone's favorite, water with a squeeze of lemon.

After three terrible nights of sleep, I awake and drink my black coffee, watch TV, and think about the food I will be eating while also thinking about the food I will not be eating.

Amazingly, people think about food constantly, but it's easy to get caught in a cycle of just "grabbing something" and tossing it down. Elite athletes plan ahead. Luckly my wife is the planner. A few days before, we bought $200 in vegetables and planned 200 different ways to prepare them. I'm reducing carbs to one meal a day and will absolutely be skipping Bagel Thursday at work.

Breaking an eating cycle isn't as hard as breaking a complete cycle of everything. Yes, stopping alcohol is difficult for many, for some impossible. Quitting steak and burgers and bacon is hard as well. A bag of potato chips is as seductive as any food item on the shelf.

Old habits die hard.

When you do something different than what you've been doing for days, months, and years, you realize the constant routine you've been in… coffee, car, work, computer, lunch.

Plus, the things you've been eating. Toast, coffee, ham sandwich etc.

Quitting Ice cream, wine, fatty meats, while also ignoring the leftover chocolates someone left in the kitchen at work is not just discipline… it requires a rewiring of the brain. The habit of eating well, or at least eating *clean*, forces one to approach things in a manner that could be considered "life altering."

There are always a few hurdles, or perhaps "humps" to get over. A few restless nights in bed, some hunger pangs, and perhaps a headache or two is to be expected. Clean living shouldn't come with such disruption, but the body becomes confused, and the reprogramming takes a little while to set in.

There's the pain of discipline or the pain of regret. I'll try the former before the latter.

Unfortunately, my poor sleep has kept me from the gym. I don't mind running with minimum food in the reserves, but at 53, a few nights of bad sleep can feel like a tequila hangover and running it out on the treadmill doesn't really work anymore.

My few days of eating light, and in some instances, eating nothing, has already screwed up my body function schedule. It had been over two and a half days before I pooped. I knew I was eating too much before, yet still on a regular shit-cycle. Alternating that intake flow has disrupted the outtake flow. I guess it's to be expected. It's happed to me before. It happens to most people. The body is adjusting to a new normal.

I heard two-time NBA MVP point guard for the Phoenix Suns Steve Nash (a very fast player) mention in a podcast that the only sugar he ate was through natural means such as fruit. I'm trying to adhere to that as well, although not entirely. Peanut butter has added sugar, but I never add sugar to anything… coffee, cereal, tea, and I never sprinkle it over any other food item, so it won't be too difficult, but avoiding cakes, and candy is paramount to the cause.

When my son ran track in school, he would consume gummy bears, recommended by the coach for energy and recovery. I never heard a coach instill candy into a workout routine, but reading up on the subject has shown that gels have quick carbs that digest rapidly. They are convenient not only in portable size, but in fast absorption into the body and help replace electrolytes. When Max mentioned it was "required" to eat gummy bears, my wife and I rolled our eyes, but we bought them regardless. Now that I'm running, I stand humbly as a hypocrite. I intend to eat them as well. It will be my only source of sugar outside of peanut butter and the occasional squirt of ketchup, and perhaps the random treat that has sugar buried inside along with other ingredients I won't read because they're either too long to pronounce or were made in a lab and I don't want to think about that kind of thing.

There must be balance. Body nutrition with enough vitamins for complete mental focus. It's not starvation, it's a holistic approach to mind, body and soul.

13

Even though I missed the gym for the second day in a row, I took the stairs up to my office – on the fourth floor. That's eight sets of stairs. Not exactly 20 minutes on the stair master, but every little bit helps. Cut a little sugar here, take an extra step there... and before you know it, you've stacked the little things to make one big thing.

The next day, Feb 20, In the throes of body detox, which entails dry lips, deep hunger pangs, crankiness, and sudden energy lulls, I return to my previously scheduled training routine. It wasn't the results I wanted. In fact, it was an almost total setback.

I thought about setbacks.

I planned for setbacks.

But I meant a *small* setback

This was almost a complete reboot. My calf, which after almost five days has not loosened, forced me into a pitiful 13:07 on the treadmill. I wasn't trying to run for speed, but

I wasn't expecting a complete fall. I felt every second of my 53 years and then some. Maybe 83 years. It was truly a demoralizing experience. Enough so that ruminations of quitting entered my head.

Friday was creeping up and I thought "Wine, burgers, couch" were exactly what I needed. I had a fourth night of bad sleep, set up by my lingering facial neuralgia which crops up from time to time. I'd kept it at bay to that point, but after a little neck stretching before bed, it seemed to activate the electric shocks on my face.

Facial neuralgia is a condition in which the nerves in the face electrocute you. It's painful, but what makes it worse is the painful shocks come unexpectedly. Literally the second my head hit the pillow the pain started, forcing me to get up and put a hot compress on my neck to alleviate muscle pressure on neck nerves. I now need compresses for my face and my calf. High and low. At the rate I'm going, I'll need to conduct business in a hot tub.

Perhaps everything is coming at once. Pain, lack of sleep, diet change and alcohol withdrawal. Maybe they're all related. They most likely are. This is where *will* and *internal fortitude* must prevail. If I get through the weekend with rest, a few sessions of running, and come out the other side healthy and feeling good, I'll know I can take a leap forward. If not, I may be on a path to stopping as quickly as I started.

Freshness is surely a problem when you're deep into a goal. I've been writing for the better part of 40 years and I love it. I began writing books earnestly about 20 years ago and published about four years ago. But that's a passion I've developed through decades of constant work. Stumbling out of the starters block on an activity that I had a passing fancy for in the first place is reason enough to stumble directly off the track. A dream and a passion can be one and the same, but a silly daydream and a passion are two different things.

I've overcome exhaustion more times than I can count. But I've never had a physical injury, nor such a disruptive state of sleep outside of being sick with the flu. The plane may land faster than it took off. Bailing at the first sign of turbulence is not the badge of honor one hopes to wear, but unless I can find smooth air, I may crash sooner than later.

I realize I've tossed around a lot of similes and metaphors; but what can I say? I'm a writer. In the future I may be a runner. Now I'm just a writer who runs... and, apparently, complains a lot.

Positive mental outlooks are essential, but getting yourself into that frame of mind is also essential. Usually, wine did that for me. Now, it must be done through meditation and inner peace. Inner peace while maintaining the fire inside is not necessarily a contradiction in terms.

Intensity and calm are the building blocks of proper balance. The Yin and the Yang. Fire must be implemented at the right time, but calm must be achieved when most necessary. I've gone to bed with my brain running in a state mania regarding future endeavors:

How I'm going to run,
when I'm going to run,
what will be my running time,
and what to eat before and after running.
Usually, my bedtime mania is about writing.
What I'm going to write,

when am I going to have the time to write,
and what am I going to do with it once I'm finished.

I've replaced writing with running. They rhyme, but are so very different. I struggle with compartmentalizing the things that need energy when needed, and the things that need calm when they are needed. I awaken for the gym in near exhaustion because I've been running my mind in bed. But when I'm at the computer to write about running, my energy practically explodes with excitement about my next training session.

My son has read books about envisioning goals and having them appear in the quiet moments of reflection. He's read books by Kobe Bryant and college basketball stars. Players who swear by the credo of quiet self-focus. Envisioning goals set. Envisioning the conquering of goals; seeing yourself accomplish them. Seeing yourself throwing the basketball into the hoop and crossing the finish line as the clock hits the desired time.

The mind needs discipline as much as the body, but there's a part of the brain that needs it as much as anything.

This particular brain chamber is hard to access. It resides in a place that can get further away as you get older, but also further away the more your world becomes chaotic. It's not easy to stop and say, "let's meditate." Sometimes it's nearly impossible.

These difficult to access mind zones require a certain magic that only the user can conjure. One must allow themselves entrance into that place, and the key to the door will not always fit. There's a certain alignment of the planets, so to speak, that need to happen for the access to happen. Once done, it can be done easier each time. But it's not so simple.

For me, mental meditation can feel a lot like sleep. I close my eyes, and my brain wants to shut down like a closed laptop computer. *Zzzzzzzz*. Closing the eyes feels like a ripe opportunity to shut the brain down, not make it work more. Sure, the body may relax a bit, but the mind needs sleep just as much, if not *more* than the body at times. What's the balance? Where's the peace? Where's the focus, and how can you train the brain to decipher the two?

The brain uses a tremendous amount of energy. Scientists say it can use somewhere in the realm of 20% of your daily energy. That means sitting around *thinking* can make you exhausted like any physical activity. It requires protein and sugar just as much as your calves and biceps. Like a small engine itself, it burns constantly – even during rest and sleep. Making it "stop" so to speak, is impossible, but it's possible to make it function more efficiently by training it to open and close at proper times. To settle it down when it needs it, and to open it up when the time is right.

Much like lacing up the sneakers and simply running out the door, the brain requires a certain dose of the same thing. Then, as time goes on, you train it like you would the body. The body stretches, the muscles build, and the lungs get bigger. The brain will invariably do the same. It will stretch, it's chambers will open, and the way you approach its focus will be determined how much of it you can conceivably handle by understanding yourself.

How far do you want to go?

How deep can you fall inside?

How far is good enough and what the hell do you do

when you get there?

Again, a setback is a setback, but it doesn't have to be total despair. A physical limitation can also be a time for mental expansion. And that is how I approach it. I'm getting to know the inner *Yin* of the mind in the time I have allotted to let the physical *Yang* of the body rest and recuperate.

14

Having finally gained (somewhat) complete focus – including mental and physical harmony; dietary balance – eating simple, clean foods and eliminating junk; excellent hydration – incorporating large volumes of water while elimination alcohol; and an injury-free body – with good stretching, recovery time, hot and cold therapy and proper technique, I dive into my training.

I stay laser-focused and work towards a benchmark that I consider crucial to keeping myself motivated through this process. I want to be at the six-minute mark by April 1st.

No, I'm not fooling.

Stop laughing.

That's 40 days.

My next mark will be the eight-minute mark and if I can achieve that in a week or so, I don't see why I couldn't hit six minutes a month after that. Perhaps I'm delusional. It wouldn't be the first time. I thought I'd be internationally famous after I published my first book. I wasn't even recognized within my own family. There are worse fates than not being world-famous. I tend to have high hopes. I've shot for the moon only to find myself still firmly planted on the ground.

I worked out my gluteus and back after my disappointing 13:07. My lower back was pinching after the workout, but not enough to stop me from pushing myself.

After I mentally recovered from the disappointing setback, I entered the gym again – legs stretched, calf recovered. I pushed myself hard and ran a solid 9:42. I didn't crack the eight-minute mark, but I ran a few different speeds to get acclimated. I ran a steady 6pmh, with a few 4mphs, a smattering of 8mphs and a quick 9mph.

The muscles on the bottom of my feet (perhaps that's the plantar fasciitis) were tight, but not enough to slow me down. Afterwards I did a leg workout.

3 sets of hamstring curls

3 sets of leg extensions

3 sets of lower back raises

3 sets of calf presses. Working both feet simultaneously and separately.

Diet:

Gluten free waffles with peanut butter; egg salad; rice; sautéed zucchini; Kefir with blueberries / strawberries / Coconut; beer; lean burgers (no buns) and salad.

Shit! Yes, I know. I had a beer.

Actually, I had two.

It was a moment of weakness. After a tough day at the office with a reoccurring bought of facial pain, I bailed work early, came home and had an ice-cold beer. Actually, I had two, as stated. Trust me, I'm more disappointed than you. I went a full five days without a drink and in one crack of the can, I tossed my drinking discipline out the window.

I will start next week fresh with a renewed sense of sadness… I mean focus!

Drinking is bad for me, I know that. I must remember that. Researching online with the subject "is it OK for an elite athlete to drink a little alcohol?" I was met with many answers, none of which I was satisfied with.

Among the problems with drinking alcohol is its ability to restrict the lungs and prevent efficient breathing. During my training, my breathing was the least problematic of all my problems. In fact, breathing and lung capacity had exceeded my expectations. I don't plan on running *while* drinking a beer, but I suppose the effects of alcohol are overarching.

For complete lung and body efficiency, I must abstain. Forget about what alcohol does to the lungs. The kidneys and liver, organs that help process toxins, must be clean and running proficiently as well.

Later, I scrolled through a RUNNING subreddit on Reddit. On one chain, an Original Poster asked, "what was your accomplishment today?" The responses were eye-opening. I was expecting "I ran four miles in one minute" or "I ran a marathon in one hour." But they were surprising in other ways. I expected it to be a chain of elite athletes, but some people stated it was the first time they ran in five years. Someone said they were injured. Someone claimed to have just started running after a stress fracture. One person admitted to not running at all.

After that dose of reality, I felt better about my minor setback. I didn't join the subreddit, nor did I engage. I didn't want to post "I ran a 9:42 mile" after someone stated they ran a mile in 20 minutes. It's not important for me to announce my accomplishments. Reddit is an anonymous place to post. I'm not trying to gloat, nor am I trying to get virtual pats on the back. I will continue to put my head down and hit my goals. No one needs to know. Especially this sorry lot.

I'm kidding!

I was once pretty sorry myself. I'm sure some guy will get on later to claim he ran 50 miles before breakfast and make any accomplishment I achieve seem trivial.

Everyone is in a different stage of competing. Some of the men my age at my gym are in way better shape than me. They have lean, runners' bodies. Their endurance is tip top. Until I can run a mile without practically dying, I have nothing to say… nothing to gloat about, nothing to boast about, and certainly nothing to post about. I've won no awards and achieved nothing other than the act of ceasing to put things into my mouth and swallowing them.

15

Next day, after a bad night of sleep, I do what most elite athletes do – I laid on the floor of my living room in the sun.

We have no furniture. The entire room is empty. We haven't purchased any furniture to fill the room because we can't afford it. The sun pours in like opens swaths of beach, so my wife and I laid down and sunbathed like vacationing in Florida. If people ask me where I got my golden tan, I'll say Casa de Schmitz. It's a hot new spot on the map. Cheap too. Practically free to get there and the cost of a room is almost zero – If you don't include taxes and bills and stuff like that.

Later, we went to the gym. My son wanted to play basketball and somehow, I played too. My day of rest turned into an hour of basketball. It's good for me. I've heard it's important to train in other sports because it helps you mentally and physically in the sport you're trying to excel in.

Perhaps different muscle movements and body co-ordination taps into a side of yourself you didn't know was lacking. My old basketball skills came back in a flash. I was rebounding like Dennis Rodman, playing defense like Rodman... and shooting like Rodman. For those who weren't alive in the 1990s or watched basketball, Rodman was an excellent all-around player outside of scoring, where he had the shooting touch of a man with frying pans for hands.

Rodman was also known to go off to Las Vegas on a two- or three-day drinking bender and come back not having lost a step. I suppose I can have the same two- or three-day drinking bender too. Although Rodman was a premium athlete – a physical freak of nature – and I'm nothing more than an average guy trying to get to an average running speed before trying to hit an elite running speed. I also hate Las Vegas, but that's beside the point. Rodman also married himself.

I know, it doesn't make sense.

He showed up in a white wedding dress and... listen, perhaps he was in love. I don't know. Sometimes you find that certain someone who makes your heart rate go up. Even if it's yourself.

My heart rate was up, that's because I moved well and was flexible. I didn't tire and my stamina lasted throughout. My son felt knee pain, which happens at times, but my knees felt very strong.

Later, after some light squats, I realized I need to improve the strength of my inner legs. Looking at a human anatomy muscle chart, that part of the body would be the Glacilis, and the Adductor Longsus... that's the muscle near my schlongus. I will also concentrate on knee strength (patella), and work on core muscle strength and flexibility (obliques and abdominis).

My food intake: Gluten free waffles with peanut butter; half pound of chicken salad; banana; roasted salmon with rice and Brussel sprouts; frozen mango with milk.

Sunday, was an actual day of rest. Besides coaching my son's basketball team to a winless season, we stopped at a bar to see my uncle's band jam on a warm winter afternoon. It was 3:00 in the afternoon and we ate some food and listened to some great music.

Food: shared mini pizza, pretzel, cheeseburger slider, fries, beer... heaping doses of regret.

Surprisingly, my son was not disappointed by the winless season. He's trying to get better and has adhered to my philosophy that the winning will come when the game is played the right way. Some of his teammates don't like that philosophy. Those are the kids who take terrible shots, play hero ball, and complain to the ref after they're fouled while the opposing player they're supposed to be defending is running down court scoring.

What can I do? They're 14. I can't make them see the big picture. Perhaps I should instill my philosophy into my running. I'm trying to change my diet, eliminate foods, hydrate, get flexible, build muscle and break the four-minute mile in a matter of weeks. I must learn the art of patience and understand that at the ripe old age of 53, this goal may take longer than I had envisioned.

16

A few days later: one mile on the treadmill. Ran an 11:11. Wasn't trying to break a record. Didn't love the time, but didn't hate it. Basketball all weekend made my legs rubbery.

Food: kefir with chia seeds and bananas, chicken cutlet, elbow pasta, grapes; chicken breast and roasted sweet potatoes. My diet will mainly consist of yogurt, kefir, fresh fruit, nuts, peanut butter, roasted vegetables, lean meats, beans, salad, the occasional potato, as well as carbs consisting of pasta or rice.

By the way, I'm convinced chia seeds do nothing for the human body. My wife keeps putting them in things, but I'm skeptical. I remember when chia seeds were used for Chia Pets – that "toy" where you'd spread chia seeds over a clay dog or pig animal and a few weeks later, you'd have a worthless green ball of sprouts growing on your windowsill. No one ever thought of eating the seeds until perhaps some dim kid ate them and his energy level rose, or he miraculously got over the flu.

Stocked with a system of carbs from the pasta and meat sauce meal from the night before, I hit the gym and ran my best mile time thus far… 8:00 minutes! ON… THE… DOT. I would have been ecstatic at the time, but I was so exhausted I nearly keeled over. A contributing factor to my amazing time other than pasta and sheer will may be attributed to *actually* tying my sneakers instead of just slipping them on. The tightness felt very nice and stabilized my footing. Prior to the run, I did a good stretch and warm up, then ran a bit to loosen the muscles.

Loose muscles, tight shoes… good philosophy.

I attacked the treadmill hard out of the gate. I ran the first quarter mile in 1:43, averaging a speed of 8 mph. I maintained that for about 10 seconds after I crossed the 1/4 mile line, then needed to slow down. The remaining run was a mix of 4mph, 6mph, 8mph, and even a dash of 9mph.

I was absolutely determined to get to the 8:00 minute mark, but it did not come without its issues. My breath was good, but I struggled with it at times. Hydration was ok, but not great. My most troubling issue was my inner knee. It didn't feel structurally sound. I felt no pain, no tightness and was overall very happy with my conditioning, but during the run I felt my knees 'buckle' for lack of a better word. Not lock-up and fall down kind of buckling, or a collapsing feeling, but the knees felt less completely connected to the entire leg system that overall was working efficiently.

I believe my leg muscles are strong, but they are "gym strong" as some people say. Meaning; muscles can be big, and strong, and look great, but they are only as good as the movements they are forced to do in a mechanical way. Body builders are big, and strong, and have big muscles, but they may not have flexibility, balance, or an overall holistic connection to every muscle those muscles are connected to. My knees need work because my gluteus needs work. I need better core strength and foot strength. Also, I need stronger muscle-attached-to-tendon connections in strength and flexibility. Running off the ball of my foot for a better "spring" requires a leaping ability that is entirely dependent structurally from the mid-abdomen down to the tip of the big toe.

I end my workday by watching a video of two British blokes talk about how difficult it is to run the four-minute mile, then proceed to break it by running downhill. I'm not sure they believed this was a legitimate win, but they seemed awfully pleased with themselves and failed to mention that it was broken by going downhill. Perhaps they assumed that we, the viewer, knew that using gravity and essentially *falling* downhill on their legs is not a legitimate accomplishment, and they do mention the speed in which one needs to break the finish line – both noticeably stunned. Stunning to me was the drone shot of an orange running track set against a grassy green field during the opening sequence which, compared to the little blue oval on the treadmill's monitor, seems strikingly colossal.

After nearly every positive accomplishment I achieve during this process, I get knocked back down to earth by some form of reality in the guise of body pain, images, or information; either coincidentally, or because I've gone down some rabbit hole internet search, looking for things about technique, exercises, equipment, or running history.

My high was proceeded by a low. Broke the 8-minute mile mark (high), see an actual bird's-eye view of the track (low). One positive I do take away from recent internet searches is someone stating that breaking the four-minute mile is "mostly about cardio." I'm not sure if that's true, but I will work on it diligently. It's something to test as I continue towards the six-minute mark

17

Of the many predicaments I found myself in over this journey, was knowing the proper time to contact the people of the "running world" to let them know I planned to break the four-minute mile; whoever those giants of the running world may be.

I figured once they heard this announcement, they'd stumble over themselves to come to the nearest track to photograph me, interview me, and even shake my hand. This kind of news is "Breaking News" as they say in the news world. Something to set the athletic world abuzz. At first, I thought it prudent to alert these people the second I came up with the idea. Later, I thought it would be wise to contact them as soon as I hit the eight-minute mark. Upon further reflection (or sobering reality), I realize it was too early for this announcement in any way.

Much like the announcement of my first book, I feared it would be met with the sound of crickets. In fact, I was assured it would be met with crickets, so I put the announcement in my back pocket until I knew I could at LEAST get to the six-minute mark.

One thing I most definitely needed to do before even that, was to find an indoor track to run. Where are these tracks? Is there a track membership? My local YMCA, of which I'm a member, has a track that is 1/16 of a mile per loop, but that's far too small and would feel like a dog circling a rug before dropping for a nap. I need distance – long spaces to open up my engines and bound like a deer running from a hunter. I want to dash and gallop like a horse.

Then I thought, before I even do *that*, why not go to my local runner's store and ask some questions to the people who work there even though I don't intend to buy anything. Workers in stores LOVE that kind of customer. This runner's store is right down the street from me, filled with people who own bulging, veiny legs. Lean guys with healthy tans even though it's the middle of winter. They have bright shoes and tight ball caps and jaws made of those stringy rubber bands from those rubber band machines I talked about. They're enthusiastic, yet also slightly crazy in a good way. Sure, they may not be able to talk about Shakespeare or the batting average of Aaron Judge, but when talk arises about rubber soles on the pavement, they salivate like a dog at a rib smoking convention.

Perhaps these runners in the know, knew where these tracks were, or where these runners' groups are located and how they can be contacted.

But there must be a limit to how many questions I can ask before they get suspicious of my intensions to buy nothing. Not only will they get suspicious, but they could also get annoyed or even hostile. Yes, they're running nuts, but they're also working on commission and probably get some kickbacks to sign people to runners' clubs and other worthless associations like that. To let a fish off the hook like me, a natural born sucker, would be a genuine loss of money, time, and brain cells.

I may need to go in and *buy* running shoes, an item I've been wanting to purchase regardless. I may go in for information and leave with sneakers. Their information may be worth the purchase. $150 sneakers for 10 nuggets of valuable information might be worth the price. I'll weigh that cost upon arrival.

My sister was in town for the weekend and my allotted single glass of Saturday wine turned into three. Examining the multiple empty bottles on the counter, I wondered "who drank all this wine?" and the answer was obviously *me* as I was coming in for a refill… probably for glass number four. But that happens in social situations. My sister and I like to chat, and wine tends to tip. So as to come across in this book as a responsible adult who makes proper decisions, I will say I drank three glasses of red wine.

The week's training went solid. Sunday basketball with Max; Running Monday; Slept in Wednesday but ran Thursday. Light neighborhood jog on Saturday. All just to keep the fitness and blood moving.

I weighed myself and didn't budge an inch up or down. A solid 179 pounds. But my gut is reducing, and my legs are noticeably stronger and thicker, as well as my butt, which is rounding into shape… no pun intended.

As I continue to point my life in the runner's direction, my social media feed, feeding off my interests and internet search algorithms, spoon-feeds me facts and tidbits about running life. Stories about sprinters, marathon tips, and philosophies populate my timelines with seemingly impeccable timing. I think about clothes, my feed displays clothing. I think about muscles, a muscle factoid appears.

At one point, a split screen image of a thin, gaunt distance runner and a thick, muscular sprint runner appears with this "fact." It's something I cannot corroborate because I have nothing to cross-reference it with. This was from *The Runner's Week*, a publication from Italy.

It stated: *"Imagine two elite runners in the same sport. One is the long-distance runner, and the other is a sprinter. The long-distance runner has a very lean build. This is because his discipline requires intense endurance work. His muscles rely on slow-twitch (red) fibers, which are lower in volume but highly resistant. These fibers enable him to maintain a high, steady pace over long periods. In contrast, the sprinter trains with explosive, anaerobic workouts. His session are short but extremely fast, building significant muscle mass that lets him achieve impressive speeds. However, his muscles consist mainly of fast-twitch (white) fibers, which tire quickly, limiting his speed to only a brief period."*

Translated into English from Italian or not, it's well stated. I found it all very illuminating. Unfortunately, I had no idea what it all meant. Red slow-twitch fiber and white fast-twitch? Sounds like James Bond defusing a bomb. Cut the red wire and there's bound to be a terrible explosion. Now I had another thing to consider. The twitch. Twitch fibers.

Perhaps it was something I've needed to know about.

But where does the four-minute mile guy fall?

Is he somewhere in the middle?

Surely, he must run fast like the sprinter, but his race lasts far longer than 10 seconds and he doesn't need those top speeds.

He must go for four minutes.

The middle runner is most definitely not on par with the marathoner. The marathoner's race lasts hours, far more than the four-minute mile guy.

What twitch muscles must the four-minute man develop?

Red? White?

This is a conundrum I usually have with wine.

The French Red or the California white.

Now it's related to fibers. Should I develop both in equal measures? Maybe I have neither; not having run much at all these past few years. Perhaps I have blue fibers. Fibers developed from weightlifting, but not much else. Is there a combo of the fibers? Red and white. How about pink? Or Rosé?

I may not need to worry about fibers at all. The less I know the better. I think in the process of my daily routine; I'm developing these things. Red. White. Fibers. Etc. Maybe the guys at the runner's shop would tell me more.

In my experience, twitchy means jumpy. Springy. fast-moving, spastic, unstable, nervous. Things you associate with the guy about to rat out a mob boss under hot lights – a snitch with a tell or a high-strung drug addict with a serious brain issue.

In relation to sports, it can be something for basketball players or ping pong enthusiasts, where movements shift rapidly, and information needs to be processed quickly. Not for straight-line running. But what do I know? I know nothing, so I'll get twitchier.

I awoke the next day to another post from another running magazine blog thing-a-ma-bob about breathing recommendations. That's something I already figured out on my own, but it's good to know I'm correct in my assessment of deep breathing with good lung and diaphragm control.

I'm also finding a large number of THC gummy ads on my timeline. I may have (definitely) clicked on an ad for weed gummies at some point and now the entire national hemp gummy industry is hounding me to buy their product. Why these things weren't available when I was a pot head is frustrating, but it's possible I'd still be living in my parent's basement if it had, although I seemed to locate weed just fine in my 20s and somehow made it through life with a good job and a family, so perhaps legalized drugs isn't the worst thing in the world. The Netherlands legalized marijuana (with heavy regulations) years ago and they're a model of good citizenship, with a functioning, healthy environment built around life balance and the bicycle as transportation. Instead of these gummy companies exhausting the value of their product on how high you can get, they push the narrative that it's a great alternative to alcohol – relieving stress, so you can awake refreshed and without a hangover. I suppose it's a fine stance to take.

My main wonder now comes from when this running will all become a treat and not chore.

Yes, I have a goal to meet and I'm enthusiastic to do it, but the runner, at some point, has the "Runner's High" kick in, without the use of gummies. They feel a euphoria that takes them to the promised land. It's a feeling they chase because they know they can achieve it again and again through the activity they love. I haven't reached that nirvana, although I've had my moments of mild bliss. Usually this runner's high is imbued to the long-distance runner. It comes at a point when the endorphins, or the body's own self-producing psychostimulants flood the blood. I'm not sure at what point it kicks in. 40 minutes? Two hours? Six months?

I don't believe the speed runner is able to get this high, but I was hoping at this point to get something in the realm of "spirit" or transcendence. Maybe I need to have spirit and transcendence come at the right times.

When I'm at my desk, I think about running, but when I'm on my way to the gym to run, all I can think about is sitting down. It's a paradox I'm having trouble overcoming.

Perhaps it's the petulant child in me: "I want to run the four-minute mile NOW!" not in four months. Impatience is the road to dreams dying. Then the other voice in me, the voice of reason says: "No! You'll train like everyone else!" I suppose if I ran every day, I'd be in a better groove, but my knees would grind to dust, so the non-running moments need to be revered as well.

18

When Harrison Ford made the movie *Indiana Jones and the Last Crusade*, he was 47 years old. I know what you're thinking... "Jesus Christmas, are you obsessed with Indiana Jones movies?" The answer is yes, but I have a point to make.

In the first film *Raiders*, which came out in 1981, there's multiple scenes of Jones running. Even at the age of 39, Ford is starting to show the signs of a man whose legs are aging. He runs with his body weight lower, more centered and careful, like a man afraid to fall. Nearly eight years later in *Last Crusade*, he runs even more like an old man. Even though Ford was in excellent shape, having trained with professional trainers to enhance his conditioning for the film, he's unable to hide his age. He runs even lower, from the hip area, back bent, with less stress on the legs. I'm older than Ford was in this film – by nearly six years.

When I first started this process, I found myself doing the same 'lower body, hip running' that Ford does in *Last Crusade*. I've had to adjust my body and train myself to run with more confidence... higher up, so to speak, on my legs and not from my hips... unafraid to get hurt and unafraid to put too much stress on the legs. It's essential to put stress on the legs to complete this task, so complete and proper strength building must go into the training.

And so far, the results have been good.

Because reading about people's food consumption is boring as hell, and reading about their daily progresses and regresses is less interesting than listening to their dreams, I skipped over a week.

You're welcome.

But, for the sake of transparency, I'll transcribe the overall events in a succinct and pithy manner.

Feb 27:
Jogged 3/4 mile
Glutes workout. Sore right Achilles.
Chicken salad for all meals.

Feb 28
Rest day.
Awoke to sore LEFT Achilles. Sleep injury?
Tight hamstring. Craving ham.
Pizza lunch. Small, accidental wine. Don't ask.
Chicken salad.

March 1
Wine regret.

Finally ate the ham I craved... with eggs.

Light jog around the hood.

March 2

Son's basketball playoff game. Slaughtered. Season over. Zero wins. Dejected.

Academy Awards on TV. No *Raiders* or *Chariots*. Have seen none of the films.

Wine regret lasts one day. Drink another.

Chinese food. 5 pigs in a blanket.

Small ice cream

Diet slowly unraveling.

March 3

Wine regret again.

Diet regret.

Total regret.

Gym. Punishment for weekend: 1 1/4 mile on tread, core workout, shoulders, curls.

Heart weak. Lungs good.

March 5

Rest day

Stretching, stairs to office.

March 6

Gym.

Mile time: 10:28

Hip pain. Leg and Glutes workout.

Chicken salad.

My latest run time is disappointing for sure. I felt good the night before. Strong. Ready to run fast. The next day I still felt good but tired. More mentally tired than physically tired.

Once at the gym and after a good stretch, I hop on one of the many available treadmills. After a burst, I slow considerably. Even 7mph is tough on the body so I reduced to 6mph and then 5mph. My hips hurt and I was stiff. Harrison Ford stiff. It's a tough run time to deal with. I knew there'd be steps backwards. I've stated it multiple times. But a 10:28 is a considerable stumble.

After a week, with multiple setbacks, cheating, weakness and poor discipline, I realize I've been approaching this the wrong way. Diving in with both feet and completely restructuring my eating and lifestyle plan was not the right approach. Yes, going cold turkey on certain things is the way to go… like cigarettes or crystal meth... not ice cream. Replacing turkey with ice cream is smart because it's healthier, but eliminating everything you love is a recipe for disaster.

This is a marathon, not a sprint. I mean, it's a sprint and not a marathon. You know what I mean! The training part is a marathon as far as its scope, and not a sprint as far as getting instant results and satisfaction. I must build in moments of failure so that I may understand it as part of a bigger picture.

Most runners need 20 weeks to prepare physically for a marathon and because I'm in good shape but NOT a runner, I need 20 weeks too. Let me make it clear that I'm running a sprint and not a marathon. But the marathon training mentality is needed. They both eat well, eliminate fatty, processed foods and run a lot. But other than one runner running far and one runner running short, they train relatively the same.

20 weeks puts me at the end of May. That's a relief, but not an excuse to screw around. I can't eat bowls and bowls of ice cream and expect a few days of treadmill training to melt it all away. But, to think I was going to knock this achievement out of the park in a month is ridiculous. Any coach tells its team when they're losing a game, "we need to do this one possession at a time!" There's no 21-point touchdown. No five-point basketball shot. No six-run home run. There must be a long view. A divide and conquer mentality.

I will give myself a cushion and focus on hitting my goal by the *end of June*.

From start to finish, the entire process is six months.

FOUR MONTHS LATER

19

Here's three newsworthy running items that happened in March:

1. The Barkley Marathon concludes without a winner

I'm not sure if you're familiar with this "marathon" but it's even more insane than the Cooper's Hill Cheese-Rolling run where people shatter their shins and twist their spines into pretzels falling down a hill. The Barkley is a 100-mile marathon over harsh, knotty terrain in Tennessee, and not many people have finished it. That's because it's grueling to run. Twisted ankles, broken knees, as well as dehydration and exhaustion overtake most partakers. Nobody finished the race this year and every picture I see on the internet, someone looks completely devastated or injured. The Barkley Marathon founder Lazarus Lake claims, "most runners should fail to complete the race as failure is essential to growth."

I agree, because I've failed at so many things in my life and I've grown... slightly.

2. 15-year-old Sam Ruthe breaks the four-minute mile mark

Later that same day, I see that a 15-year-old kid from Aukland, New Zealand named Sam Ruthe became the youngest person to break the four-minute record with the time of 3 minutes and 58.35 seconds. At this point, the next person to beat the record will be 12 years old. Fortunately, there's been no 60-year-old to break the record, making any achievement I get null and void. I don't plan to train for another seven years to break that, so it's either now (or close to now) or never (absolutely never). Not surprisingly, Same Ruthe broke the previous record for youngest person to run a sub four-minute mile, which was held by Jakob Ingesbrigtsen when he ran a 3:58.07 at 16.

3. A.J. Schmitz shatters the four-minute mile record

OK, number 3 is not true.

So now I must confess... I got to April 1st and not only did I fail to get to the six-minute mark as I had previously marked as my next timeline benchmark, I never hit the eight-minute mark again! Some of you may be shocked. Some of you are not shocked at all.

There were several factors involved in my setback.

"What were they?" you must be wondering as you sit at the edge of your seats. Well, let's review the last four months...

After a nose cold (I know, not a crippling malady) I was met with a family stomach flu which spread like wildfire through the house, causing us all to projectile vomit until we were drained of energy. *Still*, you may be thinking, *that shouldn't have set you back too much.* Then the putrid winter weather kicked in with driving sheets of frozen rain that didn't relent for weeks. Now you're saying, "You're just making excuses!" You may be right, but it was truly terrible weather.

Still, it didn't throw me off too much. The thing that really stopped me dead in my tracks (both literally and metaphorically) was a toothache.

My trigeminal neuralgia nerve affliction causes facial pain and I thought that's what a new bout of jaw and facial (and skull) pain was attributed to. My wife, whose had some serious teeth issues in her day, said to me, "I think you have a toothache!" I didn't believe her. That's because I've never had a toothache before. I've never had a cavity before! My parents instilled a militaristic ritual of teeth-brushing in me as a kid and it's prevented four out of five dentists from looking into my mouth over the years. But doing everything from chewing to brushing my teeth was causing me agony, so I finally went to the dentist.

My wife, who for months had insisted my pain was a toothache, then went into a week-long session of "I told you so" that was almost as painful as the toothache itself, but that is another story.

Our family dentist retired a year earlier to teach dentistry at Stony Brook University on Long Island. Her students would benefit from that change, but not my teeth. Because of this sudden life-changing career move, I didn't go to the dentist for a year. I finally broke down and went to a new dentist. He didn't take my insurance, but I was desperate. It's difficult to break-in new doctors and dentists because you spend a painful amount of time discussing your personal history, but dentists can see the personal history of your teeth in about 10 seconds. Your teeth are like a book. Every stick of gum chewed, every schoolyard knee to the face, and every hole drilled is there in black and white... and red all over.

After dental assistant Julie jammed that uncomfortable square plate into my mouth and took X-Rays, Dr. Magill informed me my back jaw molar was infected and required a root canal. It would only cost me $1,200. I said "go for it" even though I only had $1,000 in my bank account. I was sure once the tooth was drilled and filled, I'd have plenty of time to run to the car and escape before they knew what was happening.

Before starting, the doctor jammed a camera in my mouth and noticed the molar had actually cracked and was split into four quadrants. He said "How are you walking around with this? You must be in tremendous pain!" I said, "yeah, I guess I am." Then he said, "you must be the strongest man I've ever known," and I said, "tell that to my wife!" and we laughed until we cried...

Okay, I made that last part up – but he did wonder how I was eating and brushing my teeth in such pain. I would have told him about my gruesome training routine for the four-minute mile, a training routine twice as painful as tooth pain (not really), but at that point the Novocain was kicking in and I needed the damn tooth pulled. It took about 30 seconds to yank that thing and toss it away like a rusty nail. The bright side of the whole endeavor was it was only 900 bucks to yank the tooth, which saved me 300 smackers.

Now, what were my running successes during this time?

I couldn't eat anything for about a week other than light soups, blended fruit drinks and some boiled chicken and rice, and something amazing happened from that diet. I hit my goal weight! I lost around eight pounds, which dropped me to 171.

Serendipity!

20

The Beatles have a great song off their seminal masterpiece *Sgt. Pepper's Lonely Hearts Club Band* called a *With a Little Help from My Friends*. It's a song about how Billy Shears gets by with a little help from his friends, if that wasn't painfully obvious by the title of the song. I too got by with a little help from my friends.

First it was Alex.

Alex is a doctor. A good doctor. I know this because that's what people say about him. I don't go to him because he's a geriatric doctor. I may see him in the future because I'm getting older, but I doubt it because he's 10 years older than me and he'll be far too old to care for me when I'm old. But here's the thing. Alex is in *way* better shape than me. He's a triathlete. Those are the maniacs who run a marathon, bike a marathon, and swim a marathon back-to-back-to-back. Like, in ONE day! I'm not sure what they call those long-distance bike and swim things. A Tour? Whatever they're called, it requires a certain strength and endurance not many people have. To complete a triathlon, you need to reach deep within yourself and release a fundamental energy that pushes you over the top. You also need to be a maniac. You thought I was being funny, but I'm serious. You need to literally be insane on some level to do a triathlon.

Now that I think about, Alex might be insane. I'm glad he's not my doctor, but he's my friend, so I care for him, but like I said… maniac.

Alex did help me come to terms with something. Alex is a triathlete, but he also enjoys wine and beer. He indulges in good food and wine and balances life with pleasure. That inspired me to compartmentalize things in life, especially when it comes to training. Workout hard and enjoy the fruits of my labor. Alex (the maniac) is an inspiration to me.

My buddy Stephen (the marathoner) was also an inspiration to me. He and I decided to be running partners. His official title is not "the marathoner" like Ivan the Terrible or Alexander the Great, he just runs marathons like I spoke of earlier in this book.

He was more of that friend motivation I needed.

Stephen can run long distances, yet I can't run long distances at all. I can't run short distances either, so I'm a man without a group, but I wanted to be a better runner in general. I was worried I couldn't keep up with him on runs. We decided to go to Caumsett State Park in Lloyd Neck, New York. It's a large park with a sizable road path that circles three miles around. I know it isn't a daunting task – but intimidating none-the-less. I ran, *at most*, one-and-half miles on the gym treadmill. At times faster than normal, but still, I never ran three miles – indoor or outdoor. But training with a partner usually helps push a person further than they would push themselves when alone, so I looked forward to the motivation.

With my Yin/Yang a little out of whack, my focus a little blurry, my diet fluctuating and my doubts lingering, Stephen and I try to go for our first run. Then something happened.

Stephen went to Singapore for a month with his family and left me to train on my own.

Some friend!

I'm kidding. Still, his example of running was plenty to keep me motivated through the process. Stephen posts his runs on social media and shows where he is and how far he went. He runs here on Long Island, he runs in Singapore, he runs wherever he may be laying his head at that time. That's what a runner does when he or she has found the beauty and pleasure in running.

Even though I significantly reduced my drinking, I still sipped wine now and again while eating a new snack food. Rice cakes. Essentially, it's the worst form of cake… and rice… but it fills me up and isn't too heavy. I get the salted rice cakes because the plain tastes like Styrofoam and the sound of them squeaking against my teeth is like nails on a chalk board.

21

I must confess, I got to May 1st and not only did I fail to get to the six-minute mark as I had previously marked as my April 1st benchmark, I never hit the eight minute mark again either! Some of you may be shocked. Some of you are not shocked at all.

Wait, this sounds familiar.

What I believed to be a major issue in taking my running to the next level was the restrictions of the treadmill. I felt like an animal in a pen – caught in a confined space like a hamster on a wheel. Have you ever seen those hamsters run like crazy on the hamster wheel and eventually get caught and spun around like the spin cycle of a washing machine? That's what I was afraid would happen to me. It mentally held me back. Not only that, the bouncy nature of the treadmill and its inability to properly recreate solid ground caused me to feel strange. Anyone who has ever run on a treadmill knows the first few times you try, you feel like you're walking on the moon. Eventually you get over it, but I never could. So, I committed myself to getting on terrestrial ground and beating my time.

I began running in my neighborhood to acclimate myself to firmer ground and within a short time, I could feel the difference in my grip and foot control. My spring-step changed, but I still felt a certain sole cling to the road I never felt on the treadmill. Released from the confines of the treadmill, I was free... free to fall without flying backwards like I'd been thrown from a moving car, free to run a foot (or more) sideways without face-planting on the rolling, skin-scraping rubber "band sander," and free to fling my arms and legs without hitting the arm guards or someone's face on the treadmill next to me.

Another restriction I had to conquer was my running shoes. The gray Nike's, with my beat-up, smelly orthotic inserts were squeaking so badly, I was afraid to use them. I don't normally care what people think, but the squeaking noise the shoes were emitting were absolutely ridiculous. The Tin Man from *The Wizard of Oz* made less noise than my shoes. Especially when I wore them to any hard-surfaced area like the gym entrance, the grocery store, and worst of all, the library. The shoes sounded like someone wearing wet rubber galoshes on wrestling mats. My wife couldn't stand being around me anymore and honestly, neither could I.

It forced me go to the Runner's Shop, the sneaker shop I'd been meaning to go to for months.

22

The April showers that were supposed to bring May flowers, decided to skip April and shower down in May. I assumed June would an explosion of lush greens and flowery pinks because May was nothing but a dull gray washout. It rained just about every day... with cold, bitter air brushing against the skin and a lingering blanket of depression that hovered unabated. All physical activities (and mental activities) needed to be done indoors.

During that time, my son Max and I watched as many classics as we could. Not *The Godfather* or Lawrence of *Arabia*... the REAL classics. *Conan the Barbarian, Airplane!, Total Recall, Aliens, Robocop, Real Genius, Caddyshack, The Jerk, The Blues Brothers, Starship Troopers, Terminator 2, Monty Python and the Holy Grail, Animal House* and the entire first season of *Ted Lasso*. Surprisingly we didn't watch one sports movie with a montage, although we did consume a few Netflix documentaries about basketball, all of them seemingly produced in a matter of days, consisting of interviews with past basketball stars, all wearing the same outfit they did in the other documentaries, interviewed in the same "home" setting, and saying the same things about one another – both good and bad.

I continued to train, getting back on my feet after health delays and heaping doses of sloth. My wife noted the size and strength of my legs and lifting my shorts, I realized she was right. They were considerably stronger. My thighs had greatly increased, and my calves were thick and veiny. I also noticed the hair on my lower legs fading away. I asked my wife if I should shave my legs, and she thought that was a weird idea. I suggested that the strange, wispy hair fluttering around my pale legs was uglier (and stranger) than shaving them, but she pushed back on the thought. This wispy hair phenomenon seems to occur in men of a certain age. Whether it's from socks rubbing the hair, or the pants rubbing the calves bare, no one can say. But unless you live in a sunny climate where the legs are exposed to the sun continuously, the site of a 53-year-old man's pale, dry chicken legs, regardless of their muscularity, is enough to turn the stomach.

My routine of weights continued as well, but I noticed the creeping return of my spare tire and some atrophy of my shoulders. At my age, a few days rest from the gym turns the body to jelly. A month of hard weightlifting can hone the body into a statue, but it's completely undone after a few days off. That is truly unfair in the scheme of things, but I continued on.

I reduced my food intake and pushed my cardio training. Even though I'd come to terms with the occasional glass of wine, I found myself drinking less regardless. I don't know if that's from age, wisdom, or my brain occupied with other things, but the healthy habits had taken hold.

23

Me and my pale chicken legs walked through the doors of the Runner's Shop where Rita and I were met by not one, not two, but *four* running aficionado employees who sang "hello" in unison. I said "Wow, so many people saying hello" which elicited a chuckle. Then, the wiry dude with the tattoos scooted across the floor on his small stool and came face-to-face with another dude on a stool so they could converse, leaving a young girl to help me. This girl could not have been more than 16. She was sweet, enthusiastic and informative. At first I was apprehensive, but I tore into a smattering of questions which she fielded like a pro.

"Do these shoes have arch supports?"

"What's the difference between a training and a running shoe?"

"Are these shoes here good?"

While firing these questions at her, I snuck in, "are there any indoor tracks you can go to run?"

She said there was a track at Suffolk Community College, and she thought *maybe* at St. Anthony's, but she wasn't sure if they were available to the public. Again, she handled my questions like a pro, because I'm pretty sure she'd been asked the indoor track question before.

In-between *my* questions, she managed to squeeze in a few questions of her own:

"Do you need arch supports?"

"They're basically the same depending on what you're trying to do."

"What are your running goals?"

That's the question that always grabs a customer by the throat.

"What are your running goals?"

It kicks a question back to the runner most can't resist answering.

Their "running goals."

I was tempted to gush about the four-minute mile and my accomplishments, which aren't many, so I held my tongue. I was also tempted to ask her for the phone number of those running people I needed to announce my impending record-breaking run, but I calmed myself and simply told her I was interested in "sprinting."

Although she didn't look at me like I had three heads, she was perplexed. Sprinting? I doubt many shoppers say that. 99.9 percent of their customers are joggers shopping for 'running' shoes. It's not like Usain Bolt is dashing through the door looking for those thin running slippers the 100-meter dashers wear. So, she steered the conversation in the direction she and her fellow employees turn a stray customer – to that computer running machine that checks your feet and running style so they can best pair you with a forever home shoe.

I perused the shelf and spotted a pair of white, light grey, and cream-colored Nike's that looked like little speed boats. The reason they caught my eye was the fact I was already wearing them.

Earlier that week, I filtered through a bunch of sneakers I had purchased for pennies on the dollar six months prior at a sneaker outlet store and stuffed them in my closet. When my wife suggested I pull the sneakers out (as I'd apparently been wearing the "same pair of gray sneakers EVERY DAY for the past two years"), I knew the time was right.

By the way: I didn't wear the "same pair of gray sneakers EVERY DAY for the past two years" … it was like… 18 months. But, WHATEVER!

So, little did I realize I had already purchased a fantastic pair of running shoes I was using as every day, walking around shoes. The running store girl seemed confused (again) as I took the Nike shoe off the shelf and held it up to my foot to show that, yes, I was wearing the same pair. I stated, "I like Nikes, but I'm not married to the brand!" I'm not sure why I said that – maybe it was to continue the illusion that I was *absolutely* going to buy a pair of different running shoes – maybe the dark blue Novas or the multi-colored Brooks – and not coming in to grill her for information about indoor tracks and other dumb shit.

Rita then rescued me by saying, "C'mon, let's go," and yanked me away.

"Okay thanks!" I sang as we headed out the door, assuring her I'd "be back," just like most liars say when they don't plan on returning to purchase what they promised they were going purchase.

The next day, I took the day off from work and got a nice short haircut knowing I had perfect running shoes already. I was leaner, meaner and my hair was tight and clean.

24

Tucked in the middle of the drab month of May was a glimmer of hope in the form of bright sunshine and clear blue skies. I took the opportunity to run in my hood, stretch my legs and get a face full of sun. It was the perfect weekend to finally get off the treadmill and out into what is known as "the real world" …firm ground, fresh air, and a track that wasn't a TV screen simulation or man-made in any way. Well, maybe the paved street was man-made, but other than that – *real*.

I drove my man-made car to Caumsett State Park to Lloyd Neck, a winding 12-minute drive from my home. I arrived early, paid the fair having lacked a yearly pass, and parked. The early birds were already at the early worms… I'm talking about humans if that wasn't abundantly clear, although I'm sure the actual birds were at the actual worms as well. Caumsett is a wonderful state park, with over 1,500 acres of land to roam, ancient trees, and some wildlife preserves tucked in there for good measure. All of it overlooking

Long Island Sound. In the middle of the park is a three-mile circular track. Each mile is designated with a sign marker, and the start and beginning are painted on the road with the words Start and Finish. From mile-marker one, to mile-marker two, there's nothing but swooping valleys and painful inclines, but the book-ended miles are mostly flat and easy to run.

I had my choice of starting at the beginning and running to mile-marker one, or starting at the finish and running to mile-marker two. I decided to warm up by taking a brisk walk (about 1.3 miles in total) to mile-marker one and reverse back and finish at the beginning line. Does that make sense?

Between the beginning line and mile-marker one is a horse ranch, where horses nibble on clumps of grass and stretch their legs. Their majestic muscles and lean bodies are an inspiration to anyone passing by. As I passed, they were out and about, enjoying the early morning sun – their legs caked in mud to the knee. Some were covered with blankets and other naked as the day they were born. The sky was clear, but moisture lingered in the air as the sun steamed the weeks of constant rain. Mile one is always a nice walk/run. Many parts of it are covered with leafy hanging branches, protecting pedestrians from harsh sun and cross winds. Puddles remained, but nothing to stop me from running clean and direct.

At mile-marker one, I stretched my legs and prepared my phone with the stopwatch timer. I didn't like the idea of holding a phone while running, but my son wasn't willing to come on the lazy Saturday morning, and my wife was still in bed. To run without a phone, I'd need both my wife and son there so they could communicate with each other – one of them at the mile-marker and the other at the finish line (beginning line) to stop the watch when I crossed – both communicating via phone like handheld radios. So, I was stuck holding the phone. Again, much like the treadmill, I wasn't totally free of constraints because my hand was now locked into a grip with an electronic device, but that was a small constraint considering my legs would be doing most of the work.

I gave myself a few seconds of leeway time because once I tapped the start button, I wanted a second or two to focus on my form and hold the phone so as not to accidentally stop the stopwatch with an atomic grip.

I set myself, hit the timer, and bolted. I flew past a row of honeysuckles in early bloom, past the horses who paid no attention, and finally past an elderly couple who looked at me like I had three heads. Most people on the course are not running at top speed. I passed a few groups of people and all of them had a look of confusion; like I was being chased by a bear. In fact, I'm pretty sure that's what a few of them thought because some stepped aside, and one couple even held each other like a bomb went off. Once they determined I was running for speed, they calmed down. Maybe they also looked off into the distance to see if there were bears approaching, I'm not sure. I'm a fairly considerate runner and would definitely announce if there were bears coming down the track. I didn't think about the whole "looking like an emergency" aspect of the run at the park. A running track I understand – people running at various speeds – but not a walking path with people strolling on a sunny morning.

My breathing was good, body sound. I lost the initial burst, but managed to pull it together and finish strong. I think the random people staring at me gave me a push I wasn't expecting because I crossed the finish (beginning) with the amazing time of 7:48. That was an almost dead-on time from start to stop. I'd finally gotten over the edge.

It wasn't six minutes, but the struggle to break eight minutes was gnawing at me deeply and much like the followers of Roger Banister who broke the four-minute mark months after he achieved the goal, I felt like I could do it more often having done it once.

I left my water bottle in my Jeep and the 10-minute walk back was tough on my dry throat. Once I sat in the driver's seat and swallowed huge gulps of cool H2O, I was elated. My theory about the treadmill was correct. I was free to run free. The six-minute mark was in sight.

25

Running on the treadmill again felt restrictive, but my mental hurdles were broken. At the gym I ran an 8:22, an 8:04, an 8:11, and a 7:51.

Still, I wasn't thrilled with treadmill running anymore. I needed to continue to break free. Fortunately, June came and with it, warm summer weather. The rain popped up, but there were more than enough clear days to run outside. I'd spent so long trying to find an indoor venue to run, I didn't realize that outdoor weather had finally arrived. I visited Caumsett State Park two more times and ran a 7:44 one morning, and a 7:39 a few days later in a cooler late afternoon. Both with good breath and sound body. Back on the treadmill, my running times fell with relative ease. I nailed a 7:25 and a 7:22. I went backwards a few times with an 8:57 and an 8:41, but that's because I held off on the drive.

As my run times dropped, my diet went completely out the window. Kefir was stopped completely and replaced with Greek yogurt, but my food intake was not thought about at all. In fact, I only ate three meals a day. My mid-day snack, which consisted of nothing more than a nut, pretzel, and dried fruit trail mix blend, was eliminated completely. My evening dessert was a simple half banana. My weight dropped to 169, and my face became gaunt and drawn-out. I was never a chubby-faced person being thin all my life, but with the thickening of my legs – my face, shoulders and chest lost weight. My weight dropped lower down into my frame and my body changed significantly.

At one point, while twisting together a frustrating piece of furniture with a hex wrench, a deep hunger pang rolled through my solar plexus and I realized I may have been starving myself. At the gym my legs became stronger, but my ability to lift dumbbells over my head and bench-press heavy weight was significantly affected. My thought process about my body changed completely, without trying. Where I once had a regimented daily tracking of food intake and training times, later became nothing but go-go-go. I always consumed food like a vacuum cleaner – then food became an after-thought. Food actually became an annoyance.

"I have to eat again?"

"What am I going to eat?"

"Do I really have to eat?"

"I don't feel like making something."

Even though I was running aggressively, my calorie burn was higher than my intake. My run times dropped along with my weight. They clicked off like a clock…

7:13

7:07

7:06

And these were on the treadmill!

Then, smack-dab in the middle of June, I broke the seven-minute mark with a solid 6:55.

Even the guy running on the treadmill next to me asked, "How fast were you going?" and I told him about nine miles-per-hour, although I dropped to eight, and went up to 10 a few times along the way.

My weight dropped as well.

168

167

Then, something happened to me one morning. I had a realization while walking up the stairs to my office.

I was completely and utterly exhausted.

26

It took forever for June (and good weather) to arrive, but before I knew it, June was almost over. Between work, training, final school exams, band concerts, and AAU basketball, July was creeping up over the horizon.

Because of my multiple debilitating (minor) maladies, hectic life schedule, and other distractions, I moved my timeframe again to achieve the four-minute mark. One month. My new projection was July 31st. They say, *dedication is delaying your schedule when necessary*. OK, I just made that up. Nobody says that. But we can make it a thing if everyone is cool with it. My passion to meet the goal was high, but an unsettling fact began to creep into me. Like the little devil on the shoulder. Unfortunately, it wasn't mental or physical exhaustion. It was pain.

My knee.

My left knee to be precise.

No matter how much I stretched it, rested it, treated it, iced it or applied heat to it, the left knee nagged me with a pain I can only describe as a sharp pinch. I'm sure many know what I'm talking about. At first it was tolerable – like someone digging a knuckle into my rib. Something of that nature. But then, it became clear it was something more. Getting off the couch was becoming difficult. I'd hop up from a sitting/lying position onto my feet and I could tell it was structurally unsound.

While my son beat me over the head playing basketball in my sister's pool one day, I complained of Achille's tightness and my sister informed me we inherited our father's Achilles tendons. My father, not more than four years before, blew out his Achilles, then walked around and played golf on it for a year, *then* had surgery… about a year later than he should have. I don't have that issue, but perhaps we have family leg issues in general.

The knee pinch became a pang, which then became a stab. The frustrating part was the pain would come and go. I'd say to myself, "I'm fine, it was temporary," then a few days later I'd stand up and feel as if someone notched a dart into my kneecap. And I'm not a glutton for punishment; I'm at a crossroads in life where I must decide if current pains will linger in my older age. Knee pain at 23 can be shrugged off… at 53, it can be daunting. My buddy Greg, three years younger than me, has already had hip replacement surgery, and a good number of people I know, both young and old, have replaced parts of their body with high-carbon fibers, military-grade metals, and space-aged plastics. That's the beauty of modern medicine and science, but if I can prevent that sort of thing, I will. And for the first time since I started my four-minute mile journey, real doubts began to set in.

On June 26th, the day my son finished his final exam, the school year officially ended, and the Summer "officially" began (in our house at least), I catch a news story about Faith Kipyegon, a middle-distance runner from Kenya who attempted to be the first woman to beat the four-minute mile at a Nike-sponsored "Breaking4" event in Paris at the Sébastien Charléty track. She crossed the finish line at 4:06.42, almost 7 seconds over the time. It was her personal best, but she fell short and looked exhausted from the achievement. I didn't know she was going for the record. I seem to catch these running news events when they are finished and in the public consciousness.

The news stated repeatedly that Kipyegon would have been ineligible for the record because the event was an "exhibition," which is not legitimate. I'm not sure what kind of bullshit that is, because if people are in attendance witnessing the event, using their eyeballs and noting the achievement with clocks that mark the time to the millisecond, I would think the record would stand, but I guess I'm wrong.

Kipyegon is etched in lore having won multiple Olympic gold medals in Paris, Tokyo and Rio in the 1,500 meter event. Her skills are far superior to mine. She is an absolute running machine, with a svelte body and astonishing running mechanics.

That evening, while watching a TV show we recorded on our DVR, we catch a video log, or perhaps it's a commercial (something we were supposed to skip over) about Kipyegon and her goal to beat the four-minute mile. She's running hard, training on a treadmill with her face attached to an oxygen mask and tube. She's an absolute badass. The video is enticing us to tune-in and watch her break the record. Knowing that she already failed is deflating as I watch the past and experience the future simultaneously.

Her defeat feels like my defeat as well.

What began to happen as I loosened the reins of my personal goal of defeating the four-minute mile, was a renewed grip on the reins of being a runner... in the cosmic sense. My daily routines of hammering the pavement with blunt force, turned into calm paces where I entered the flow of a run... easing into it like a boat into the water... calmly, like a leaf in the stream. The days of tackling my routine and champing at the bit to defeat another time-check faded away into peaceful runs where the mind broke free. The treadmill became my friend. So did that darn "real world." The light rain drizzles, the humid mornings, and chilly winds were welcoming and not deterrents. I embraced the random weather. I stopped complaining about the temperature and the misty clouds. In fact, I stopped checking my weather app altogether. My wife would ask me, "what's happening with the weather?" and I realized I hadn't checked it in days. Weeks even. That's the freedom I'd been looking for. The mental peace one finds on the open road. The place where weather means nothing and running means everything.

27

July 6

Two days after the fourth of July barbecues amid lingering firework bangs, I sit resting on the couch on an early Sunday morning thinking about my four-minute mile journey. Where at one point my enthusiasm was at 100 percent, now, for the first time since late December of last year, my enthusiasm has fallen well below 50 percent. The finish line, which kept coming closer and closer into view, suddenly stopped and regressed into the distance.

What started as a silly fantasy and daydream... something I truly believed could happen with nothing but sheer determination, has puffed away like a cloud of smoke. And maybe the dream is still possible if I continue, but I'm not sure I can. Pushing the timeline another month is doing nothing more than kicking the can down the road. How many times can I push the finish line? August? September? October? How about next summer? What difference does it make? I simply don't think I'm capable of achieving this goal at my age.

My philosophy of having less wear and tear on my body and knees has gone out the window. I now believe that not having conditioned myself as a running machine from a younger age has been more of a hinderance than help. I'm not built for this type of achievement. If you saw me you'd think, "you're built exactly for this type of achievement," and you'd be right. But champions are built like the towering skyscraper. They form a foundation, frame it with solid materials, and cover it in sustainable coverings. I haven't done that. Running the way I want to run is a lifestyle I've not built into my daily life. Running is life, but so is life itself. My family, my job, my writing, and my house are my life. To make running my life is to make it my absolute focus and that is simply not feasible without giving something up – perhaps giving up multiple things. My wife wants to get throw pillows for the outdoor furniture I hexed together, and instead of thinking, "that will cut into my training time," I think, "sure, that sounds nice." The comfort of time with her, the lazy Sunday at the movies with my son are the things I'll remember much later in life than any sweaty run I took on a humid summer morning.

These are easy things to reflect upon as I sit under a blanket drinking coffee while the air conditioning blasts over me by the bay window, which is dripping with dew from outside humidity. I may have regrets later for letting the passion get away – I already feel that way. There's the pain of training or the pain of regret for not meeting the goal. But, regret comes in many forms. Some of those regrets are losing time with loved ones, yet time to oneself is also important. I've felt free and focused running alone – caught in free emotions and introspection. The loneliness of the long-, short-, and middle-distance runner is not loneliness, it's the achievement of Zen. It's an inner peace that you reach when the body and mind break free, the beat of the feet on the ground becomes the drum beat you follow as your heart propels the blood through the system until you feel nothing at all… only a mental and physical flow that never ceases until you finally come to a rest. That's a place only the runner knows. Others have achieved that spiritual place in their disciplines – whatever that discipline may be. Yoga. Martial Arts. Thai Chi. Music. Fishing. Drunken full-contact chess. The runner escapes in a way that leaves them free because their running pace lets them escape into a dimension that is crossed once the air hits the face and the pulse rises. It becomes an addiction – a daily shot of endorphins that is not replicated from another source. Not *easily* that is. The skydiver fuels their adrenalin, and the drug addict satiates their pain, but the runner travels through space and time… becoming a ghost on the trail of life on the way to their destination, whatever that destination may be. It could be to nowhere – or even better – coming back home again.

Isn't that the best?

28

July 15

After a good treadmill run and aggressive workout, one in which I strain my left abdominal muscle, I sit at my desk and see another sobering news item from the world of running. Fauja Singh, AKA the Turbaned Torpedo, who was believed to be the world's oldest marathoner, died after he was hit by a car at the age of 114 while crossing the road in his native village near Jalandar in Punjab India. It's unfortunate a runner of his stature died, but more disappointing because it was at the hands of an automobile – a runner and bicyclists worst enemy. Although sad news, I was tickled by the fact this news release came via his London-based running club and charity *Sikhs in the City*, perhaps the best play on words I've seen in a very long time.

July 25

In honor of the Turbaned Torpedo and other famous runners long gone – runners who have broken records, made history, and missed the mark by seconds, I go to the local high school where my running journey first began – the place where math stumped me both physically and mentally. It's a steaming hot Friday. 92 degrees. The weather is the exact opposite of my first frigid visit almost two and a half years ago. The heat is blasting off the orange particle material like microwaves, and the fields are thirsty from lack of rain.

The track is completely empty; not only because it's too hot to run, but because school is out for summer and there's that abandoned, ghost town feeling schools gets when school is out for summer. There's no energy in the nearby building, the baseball fields have overgrown tufts on the in-field, and even though the bleachers are raging hot, they're ice-cold from lack of butts in them. Because I'd spent so long thinking about an indoor track, I never thought to return to the school until now – a month after school was dismissed. It was almost a revelation to remember the track... like a gift that suddenly appeared.

As I come to the conclusion of my running journey, the track visit truly feels like the end. Where before I wanted to know, feel, and understand the track – its mathematical measurements – its grip on the shoe soles – and partake in its grandiose rotation, I now feel no connection to it other than as a thought I seemed to misplace while thinking of other things... a roadside attraction I passed like a million other roadside attractions going someplace I actually wanted to be.

To add insult injury, I hurt my Achille's Tendon running up the stairs to my office on Monday, rendering me gimpy. I'd never really had an Achille's issue before, but I suppose the curse my sister warned me about has cropped up when I least expected it.

My wife Rita is with me at the track, and I run one quick lap while she shelters from the raging sun behind a fence banner. I do the lap in excellent time, which really sparks my soul, but to do it three more times seems impossible. I'm wearing one of my signature training outfits – the gray race car shirt my buddy Stephen designed and silkscreened, my new cream and white Nike running shoes, and my gray, ball-hugging women's running shorts with nifty yellow trim. Rita takes a picture of me. It's the image on the back of this book.

July 31

On the day I had slated to conquer the four-minute mile, I instead get into a car to visit my sister at her new lake-house on the shores of Lake Winnipesaukee, New Hampshire. From door-to-door, it's a six-hour trip. Once we zip out to Port Jefferson and catch the ferry to Bridgeport, Connecticut (on the jauntily named P.T. Barnum) and hit the open country roads (and grinding traffic), there's plenty of time to contemplate my running journey.

While my wife's bare feet rest on the sunny dashboard and my son Max bops his head-phoned head in the backseat, I accept that I'm not in any position to judge people by the expectations they fail to meet. Building a roster of athletes and guiding them to a championship must be one of the most difficult projects anyone can be assigned. Leading the New York Jets, The New York Knicks, or any major sports franchise should be left to those who know what the hell they're doing and not some armchair quarterback like me yelling at the TV. Any basketball player who misses a free throw in a crucial moment should be forgiven because God only knows what I would do in the same situation. Probably miss the entire rim, or even worse, soil myself. It takes a certain steel resolve to reach athletic goals. I now accept that I've tried and failed to accomplish even the simplest tasks of not only running fast, but setting down a cheeseburger and glass of wine, and ignoring it.

Sitting on my sister's deck above a descending hill to the shore, I drink in the lake's cool breezes while drinking a glass of red wine. I can see all those famous runners who came before me as they run across my imagination... in a movie montage sequence of course! I've never actually seen any of them run in real life, so I imagine them splashing on the beach just like the runners do in the film *Chariots of Fire* – Roger Bannister, Hicham El Guerrouj, Jakob Ingebrigtsen, the Turbaned Torpedo, Faith Kipyegon, and that old Irish bloke Eamonn Coghlan, and me lagging far behind with a soaking-wet Irish setter nipping at my heals. I raise a glass to them all.

My mind has finally settled. My dreams have morphed into other goals.

There's always another goal to achieve.

Watching the people frolic in Lake Winnipesaukee... swimming, jet skinning... the occasional boat slipping by, my mind wanders to achievements big and small. I'll publish this book, but what about… I don't know… another running event?

The New York City Marathon is in a few months.

Hmmmm.

Fine, I won't make that one, but after a long winter stuffing down cheeseburgers, I could jump into January with a renewed vigor and prepare myself for the NEXT New York City Marathon. I'll gobble down kefir with chia seeds, unseasoned chicken breasts, and vintage pinot noirs from France, then adjust my technique for the long-distance run. I'll lace up my shoes tight, stretch my hamstrings, and get my twitch muscles in tip-top shape.

Yeah… a marathon. That sounds like something I could do.

Who has the fastest marathon time in my age bracket?

Part 2
Other Delusions

FORE!

Whenever I play golf with my parents, which is very rarely, they always say the same thing... "Holy shit you suck!"

Actually, I'm kidding. They say the opposite. They say, "My god! You could have been a great golfer."

And I believe they may be right.

Then my parents look at me like many parents look at their wayward children and wonder what could've happened had they become a doctor or a lawyer instead of milking cows on a dairy farm, or blowing glass into marijuana pipes. They get that long, wistful look in their eyes, calculating the staggering array of future possibilities that washed down the drain along with the other dreams they had for me; each complicated scenario flashing before their eyes and then disintegrating into dust... the million dollar paychecks, the TV commercials for luxury automobiles... the long walks on rolling, neon green hills as the fans burst into feisty, yet polite applause.

Golf isn't really that difficult. At least for me. You take a stick with a bulbous metal thing on the end (occasionally it's wood) and smack a white ball into a hole. Sometimes the ball goes right, sometimes it goes left, and once in a while it goes straight. It's not that complicated. I can usually do it straight when I want to. The problem is the consistency. I can be the "next Jack Nicholas" on holes 2 through 5 (hole 1 being the obligatory hole in which I muff every shot because I haven't played in three years) then by hole 6, I'm playing like Jack Nicholas's neighbor Bill Stedman, the fat-ass who invented some plumbing device that made him millions of dollars, but also fueled the ice cream addiction that caused his weight to balloon with his wealth. Eventually my frustration and exhaustion take over (even though I'm driving a golf cart), which forces me to pick up my ball on hole 8 and say,

"screw it, let's get a cocktail."

Forget about playing 18 holes. That's *really* exhausting. I'll be dead by hole 11. There's a refreshment stand at my parent's golf club near the halfway point. I like to park there and drink cold beer while everyone hacks away like lumberjacks in the sand trap on 14. That terrible trap has a lip that jams everyone up and forces them shoot back towards the tee… the place a golfer is supposed to be hitting *away* from. Nothing says defeat like knocking your ball in the opposite direction the course intended you to play. It signifies all the things that have gone wrong in your life up to that point.

The thing about golf is, the more you love it, the more it will break your heart. Kind of like the guy who loves the hot dancer at the strip club, who in return wants nothing to do with her clientele because she needs to go home and feed her kid. The love is rarely returned. Anytime someone has a passion that becomes their profession, it grates the soul till there's nothing but hate at its core, even though the love is still there. That sentiment goes double for golf. You can have a lifetime of passion for the sport, and the next thing you know, you're cracking expensive clubs over your knee like campfire kindling. It's *that* frustrating a sport. You could be playing a perfect game, everything falling... the birds chirping... the sun setting on 18, and the next you know, you're screaming bloody murder at an object the size of an eyeball while cursing the gods like a sailor on shore leave. And I mean *all* the gods. The gods of the sun, the gods of the earth, as well as the gods of lightning and fire. All of them complicit in making a golfer's life miserable.

Of course, everyone comes back the next day to try it all again.

Sometimes I put golf on TV, which for some people is like watching a glacier move. I really enjoy its slow pace. I get it – it's a sloooow moving sport. It's like watching old people fuck. It's a series of stops, starts, stepping back and analyzing the holes. But for me, I enjoy the clapping. The golf clap is one of the most soothing sounds in the world. It's like white noise. It's a bunch of white people clapping so it's white noise on more levels than one. The gentle tapping of fingertips against open palms is like a sedative to me. Clap clap clap. Like rain falling on canvas tarps or the electric fan buzzing in the window. The announcers conversing quietly is very soothing as well. They whisper very softly, which can lull you into a stupor. I'm not sure why they're whispering. They're in a TV booth about 300 meters from anyone golfing, so it's unnecessary. Perhaps it's a quiet sport all around. A constant hush. They grew up around golf and everyone had to be quiet while someone was playing. In no other sport is everyone in attendance expected to be so quiet so often. You go to a football game and people are literally screaming at the top of their lungs for three hours. In golf, you're forced to whisper like a troop of nurses patrolling the newborn baby ward. Even the douche bag who screams "get it in the hole!" atop his lungs when any leader drives off the tee finds himself tranquilized by the majesty of the sun hitting military-trimmed grass on a mild summer afternoon.

The problem with golf on TV is the commercials. I'm not really their target audience. Yes, I'm an older white guy, but I'm fairly poor. They advertise wealth management groups, investment portfolios, and banks. Things I know nothing about. Basketball and football is base-level stuff. They scream about sizzling burgers and soda at hip hop concert-levels of mania... chicks with big tits draining beer down their throat... things most people understand. Some guy in a cap and farmer's tan telling me about the grip percentage of his pitching wedge or the return on investment of his 401K is lost on me.

Golf is an expensive sport. Anyone can buy a $25 basketball and hit shots at the local elementary school, but golf requires costly equipment and a million acres of space to play it. Usually that kind of acreage requires fees. Many people join golf clubs for that reason. I once had dinner with clients who debated the benefits of having a personal versus corporate golf club membership while I was wondering when to use the 10% off coupon at my favorite Chinese restaurant. If I ordered in a timely manner, I'd get the large spareribs for free, but then I'd have an extra cocktail at the bar when I picked up the order, making it a wash.

Tiger Woods is a once-in-a-generation player. You don't see lots of diversity on the putting greens. It's a rich person's game. Occasionally someone breaks through, but to properly nurture a golf game, you need cash. Buying sneakers for a growing child is hard enough; can you imagine buying a new set of clubs every six months? It's staggers the mind. My son grew five inches in a year. In club length terms that's $850. The clothes are expensive too. A normal collared golf shirt is 15 bucks, but slap a golf logo on it and it inexplicably becomes $185.

I'm not really a fan of golf fashion. It's pretty dry. Pressed shorts and Polo shirts are like vampire's garlic to me. I own those things, but I only wear them when I play golf or do things that are similar to golf – like eat at a golf club or attending an event that seems like golf but is not golf. You probably know what I mean. I can't really think of an example, but it's sort of built in by nature. At Christmas I wear red and green, at easter I wear pastels, and for golfy things I wear golf clothes. Every other day of my life I wear a t-shirt with something stupid printed on it, most likely a logo for an event someone else went to and gave to me because they wouldn't be caught dead in it. Many of my golf shirts are like that. They're nice shirts but have logos for testicular cancer charity runs, or some design that's actually cool, but ruined because it also has the logo of a giant wealth management group on it... a wealth management group that advertises during the U.S.

Open. You'll see their obnoxious logo 8,000 times during the four-day weekend tournament on TV. But regardless, I have some golf clothing staples in my closet like most people have a jacket and tie, or shoes that need to be shined with a brush and wax.

Some people are gender-fluid. I'm golf-fluid. I'll honk an obnoxious cigar and drink booze on every hole at the public course with the slobs of society, then pull myself together and drink highballs with the CFO of a hospital at the country club without skipping a beat. It's important to touch on all levels of society. If you can relate to every character in the film *Caddyshack*, you're either very worldly or a back-stabbing traitor. I like to think I'm the former, but I probably lean toward the latter. The truth is, these people are more similar than they realize. The reason being is they're all a bunch of lousy drunks. Every single one of them. The caddies and the club members think they're worlds apart, but open a fifth of scotch and suddenly they're best friends. They'll discuss the hole placement on 15 and the giant tree that drives everyone nuts on 8.

When I was a kid, I had a sports book with a story about how famous golfer Lee Travino defeated a guy using nothing but a Coca Cola bottle. I'm not sure if it's true, but a story like that doesn't start without heavy drinking involved… and betting of course. If you're losing to a golfer who's using nothing but a glass bottle as a club, you should probably quit golf. And drinking. And betting too. Travino was one of the best, but still – a bottle?

Golf is one of the few sports where you can smoke and drink as you play. Bowling is the other. Sometimes alcohol benefits the golfer. A strong buzz can do wonders for your short game. You would never see a basketball player nipping a beer on the sidelines during a game, or a football running back with a smoking stogie poking through his facemask as he plows into a defensive line; but if you're trying to sink a 40-foot put on the coastline of California, no problem. Golfers (and bowlers) are not exactly shining examples of fit athletes. In fact, a dense beer gut and back fat can really give the ball some distance. Toss in booze and cigarettes and anyone can be either a prime candidate for a major cup trophy or cardiac arrest.

Somehow these shlubby chubsters have incredible endurance. I challenge anyone to walk 20 miles over four days while swinging a metal club through tall grass 300 times as hard as you can (give or take a few dozen swings based on your talent level). If you awaken Monday morning lucky to find you haven't thrown out your neck, you'll discover you twisted a muscle in your rib cage, calf, shoulder or wrist and many other places you didn't realize you had muscles or the ability to feel pain. I once nearly snapped my forearm in half hacking my ball out of dry, knee-high grass, only to discover on the green that it wasn't my ball at all. I went from playing a gleaming, brand-new Titleist, to a dirty, chipped 12-year-old Callaway. That's enough to send me to the 19th hole (club house bar) straight away.

My father was a caddy when he was a young. He brings that up once in a while. Actually, all the time. He used to carry two bags at a time and do two loops. That's two rounds of 18 holes in one day. One loop in the morning and one in the afternoon. Honesty, that's impressive. I probably couldn't do one loop with one bag. Mainly because when I was his age, I weighed 90 pounds soaking wet and my shoulder bones popped against my skin like a starving street dog. My dad was slightly beefy. I wasn't. My father is a golf lifer. When he wasn't caddying for people at the club, he was hacking in the fringes before most people knew what golf was or could potentially be.

When I was a kid, my father and I played golf together, but I gave up when he started giving me advice during my backswing. The backswing is when you lift the club back to drive the ball forward. Talking in someone's backswing is the ultimate no-no. For some reason my father thinks it's an open opportunity to discuss any number of interesting and complicated subjects – my golf stance, my forearm angle, and my sexual orientation. I remember when I was 15, my father pointed a stern finger at me on the green at 6 and said, "I don't care who you have sex with, just use a condom." I said "OK." It was a fairly progressive statement from my Boomer father. A life lesson about sex with his son wasn't exactly his forte, but it was better than other dads I suppose… dads whose sons had knocked up their 10th grade teacher or their cousin. When he looked into my eyes, I think he knew I had some things figured out already, but I appreciated his advice none-the-less. I assumed his statement gave me the freedom to screw anyone I wanted, and I may or may not have done that as my life moved forward… but that's a different story. This one is about golf… a sport where you swing a shaft around and try and get a ball in tight hole. The sexual innuendos are endless. Basketball has a few… slamming a ball down; football with their tight ends... tennis with their love. But golf seems ripe for double entendres. There's shafts and holes and strokes.

There are many *many* joke books filled to the brim with jokes about golf. Most sports have a few jokes here and there, but golf has something close to a 50-volume set. I believe it's because golf jokes help take away the pain of playing the sport poorly. Never before have people spent so much money to be so miserable and frustrated. Perhaps at the strip club I referenced earlier, but at least in there you get a few eyeballs full of tits and ass. Golf, as they say, is a "good walk ruined." It offers very little return, and any auxiliary thoughts of breathing clean air and smelling fresh cut grass as leisure therapy are raked away in a fury of explosive aggravations. Golf on paper seems so easy to handle but you can spend a lifetime trying to master it and accomplish nothing more than looking like an idiot. There's nothing left to do but smile and hope tomorrow produces a better round.

But it probably won't.

Everyone Was
Kung Fu Fighting

When I was in the second grade, a girl named Katie ran up to me on the playground, huffing for air, and asked if I knew karate. For some reason I said yes. I could see the anguish on her face when she asked me this very specific question. She'd obviously been mistreated by school yard bullies or perhaps, a pack of samurai intent on overtaking her village, and I felt an immediate and completely irrational obligation to defend her and her people's honor with my mastery of the martial arts.

She turned, bolted, and I followed her – my hands knifed up like I was prepared to splinter wooden boards in half. She eventually stopped in a circle of kids, turned, and placed her hands on her hips. I entered the circle like a ninja, ready to pounce on the person who besmirched her name. I looked around at the gaggle of children, most of them my friends, and all of them stared at me in total confusion. Apparently, no one could figure out why the karate kid was blocking their conversation with his hands flattened before his face like a mime holding an invisible box.

Katie went into a spiel about who the culprit was, but by that time, everyone's attention was on me. They were fascinated by my karate skills, which amounted to nothing more than aping a few Saturday morning Shaw Brothers Kung Fu films I caught on channel 5.

"Are you a black belt?" someone asked me.

"Yes." I heard myself saying, my eyes bugging more intensely, as if that was part of my ritualistic training.

It was not only a pitiful display of lying, but I went with it so completely and without shame, that it started a mad decent into lying, which lasted years, and if I'm being honest, decades.

"I'm a black belt too!" Ben stated.

Suddenly, Ben and I were facing off, the two of us circling one another, hands guarded and ready to see whose technique was better.

Of course, no one on the playground questioned whether we'd practiced martial arts or not. Stick your hands up like Bruce Lee and everyone gasps in anticipation. We were seven. Seven-year-olds believe anything, including their own bullshit. Unless a sensei is in the delivery room and starts karate training immediately after exiting the birth canal, gaining the rank of black belt at the tender age of seven is a very rare occurrence.

Ben and I parried and thrusted a few times, but were rescued when the teachers called us back inside from recess. Our karate expertise was never mentioned again, nor tested in any way, shape or form. Not by me, Katie or Ben.

To dispel any notion that I was some kind of fraud, I eventually did study martial arts. When I was 14.

My mother gifted me lessons for my birthday and before I knew it, I was in a dojo, learning the ways of the defensive arts. I studied Ju-Jitsu, which is the Japanese martial art which both Karate and Judo derive. I entered the dojo as a meager, yet enthusiastic white belt, and was met with the realization that to become a black belt, it would take more than verbally falsifying my skills in a school yard scrum. It would take focus, training and consistent studies. I was hooked from the moment my sensei tossed me across the room.

Jiu Jitsu is a combination of striking, kicking, arm bars and throws. It's a style that's great for those who enjoy not only punching and kicking people, but for those who enjoy breaking people into pieces and tossing them. I emersed myself into the art and dedicated myself completely.

My sensei was easily the most unassuming martial artist you could meet. Pull any Asian chop-socky film off the shelf and there's bound to be a protagonist who on the surface appears to be no more than a common citizen, and, dare I say, someone easy to pick-on, yet when provoked, opens a giant can of whoop-ass on the unfortunate knuckleheads pushing their buttons. These unsuspecting "victims" are white-haired old men who can destroy half a gang with their feet.... the goofy kid who turns out to be a one-man wrecking crew... and of course, the dainty woman who, to everyone's astonishment, can wield every stabbing weapon known to mankind. All of them nothing more than a movie cliché at this point, yet none of them comparable to my sensei... Sensei Joe.

Even back in 1986, Sensei Joe was a multiple-degree black belt in multiple arts – Jiu-Jitsu, Judo, Karate, Kung Fu, Aikido and Kempo. Today, there aren't enough degrees to wrap around his belt, his teachings went so deep. Everyone who filtered through the door expected to see someone resembling either the square-jawed maniac Sensei Kreese in the hit film *The Karate Kid*, or his nemesis, the wise Asian sage Mr. Miyagi. What they got was someone more closely resembling Dr. Julius Kelp AKA Jerry Lewis in the hit comedy film *The Nutty Professor*. Fortunately, Sensei Joe spoke more like his dashing and confident alter ego in the film Buddy Love. And why wouldn't he be confident? Sensi Joe could kick anyone's ass six ways from Sunday and twice on Tuesday. The man was certifiably lethal.

I'm sure in some ways Sensei Joe enjoyed the secret hidden power that camouflaged his modest exterior. A Superman bubbling under the nerdy Clark Kent. I'd occasionally see him walking through town on his way to lunch; his square, steel-rimmed glasses pressed into his face and striding with the gait of a man with church-bell balls. Like he just dismounted a bronco and was heading into the saloon to whet his whistle.

One day I saw two teens making fun of him as he walked by. They mimicked his bow-legged walk, and I shook my head. If only they knew the power the man wielded, they would have kept their mouths shut.

Initially, Sensei Joe was tough on me. In his mind, it was his job to eliminate any and all pretenders who'd flooded his dojo the previous two years... fools led to believe that martial arts could be absorbed through daily chores presented in the charming yet completely preposterous film *The Karate Kid*. Apparently, the movie was a major thorn in his side. He had to instill into everyone that the only way to dismantle a crew of bullies was through bruising discipline on the mats... not because you spent a week and a half buffing car bumpers and sanding decks. I had to prove my worth and successfully navigate his tests, which meant having my ass perpetually kicked. I took the class with adults and older teens. There wasn't a kid's class. I got tossed around like a rag doll. Sensei Joe would occasionally end some of his classes by lining his students up in a queue and have them attack him one by one, defending himself using every conceivable move till he was dripping with sweat. Most people end their day with a full glass of wine and some Jazz music, but this was Sensei's way of blowing off steam. He would also test new students by singing The Human League's hit song *Human* repeatedly till we went half insane, changing to the lyrics to "They're only white belts, born to make mistakes!" I don't know what was worse, the bruises or the shrill singing, but once I got past the first month, Sensei Joe knew I was in it for the long haul.

A former pizza place in the middle of town, our dojo was exactly what you think of when you picture a Japanese dojo in your mind, except it was right in bustling Huntington village. It was a small, charming, stand-alone shack made of wood, painted white with no signage what-so-ever. It had a crooked roof, a big picture window and a few parking spaces out front. Sensei Joe gutted the place and laid mats across 90 percent of the floor. It had a training area, a bathroom and a changing room the size of a closet and nothing more. I loved that place. It was warm, bright and the perfect size for small, intimate classes.

My Jiu-Jitsu group consisted of four mainstays including me. Tony, a lanky 17-year-old who looked like Keanu Reeves from *Bill and Ted's Excellent Adventure* and John Travolta from *Saturday Night Fever* had a baby; Renee, a petite blond bookkeeper who looked 17 but was actually 27; and Brian, a big John Candy-type except in better shape and less funny. Students came and went all the time, but the four of us were the consistent crew. The core four. We trained three nights a week.

Both Tony and I got a crush on Renee. One evening she drove me home and I asked her on a date, not realizing the age difference.

"How old do you think I am?" She snorted.

"I don't know… 17?"

"I'm 27!"

"So, I guess that's a no?"

I was a brave kid. I didn't have the guts to ask girls out in my high school, yet found myself smitten enough to ask Renee on a date. Mainly because we usually trained as partners in class because of our size – consistently punching, kicking, flipping and grappling with each other. It was inevitable I'd get a crush. It would have been a convenient situation as well. At least for me. She owned a car and had a house. Unfortunately, she wasn't interested in 14-year-old boys. Nor was she interested in 17-year-old boys either. Tony asked her out a few months later and was denied. To commiserate our misery, Tony and I began to hang out.

One day Tony picked me up in his mud-colored Pontiac Coupe, a car that weighed close to two elephants. While cruising around town, Tony accidentally slammed into the back of a Honda, crushing it into an accordion. Tony wanted to leave the scene, but I told him he had to do the right thing and stay. Tony hit the Honda so hard, it crushed the doors shut, trapping the three, frail septuagenarians inside, which had to be pried open by fire-men. He got into major trouble with his parents and the insurance company. He blamed me for making him stick around when he wanted to flee. I tried to reason he could have been in more trouble had he been caught fleeing the scene, but it was for naught. After the incident, we became more distant, and I would go so far as to say maybe even enemies. Not enemies to the point we had a last karate battle at the Under 18 All-Valley Karate Championship Tournament in California, but it was an icy cold relationship soon after. Eventually, Tony confessed he was more interested in Kung Fu and soon switched over to Sensei Joe's Kung Fu class on the Monday/Wednesday Schedule.

After a year and a half of training, Sensei Joe informed us he was moving his dojo a few streets over to another location. It was disappointing because the dojo was so serene and the new location so confounding. The new spot was an awkward space on the second floor of a building above a flower shop, a converted apartment with two main rooms.

To say we drove Gloria, the owner of the flower shop crazy would be an understatement. If you thought sharing a ceiling with neighbors who danced and clopped around like horses was annoying, imagine what 175-pound men crashing to the floor all day like football linebackers sounded like. Gloria's lilies trembled like an earthquake and her potted plants swayed like a ship on rough seas.

Even though Tony drifted to Kung Fu, another enemy took his place in Jiu Jitsu class. Keith.

Keith wasn't the enemy of mine alone. Oh no. he was the enemy of *everyone*. A former US Marine advancing on his black belt, Keith was the very definition of unhinged. Aggressive to the point of mania, everything about him was crazy. He had a military buzz-cut, and the teeth-gnawing, jaw-flexing hostility of PCP addict in need of 300 CCs of high-grade sedatives. He talked aggressive, trained aggressive, and sparred aggressive. When doing something as simple as air punch warm-ups, Keith would snap his arm so hard, you thought for sure his humerus would dislocate from his shoulder like a well-boiled chicken leg off a carcass. Unfortunately, his overly combative attitude was meted out to his fellow students. Whereas Sensei Joe would use his students as training partners, Keith used his fellow students like rubber fighting dummies. Sensei Joe would constantly ask Keith to back off as he'd invariably put a 90-pound female in an aggressive choke hold, toss an unsuspecting 60-year-old against the wall, or throw me to the ground like a sack a winter salt. No one, regardless of age, sex or ability was exempt from his wrath.

One evening, after a particularly long day, Sensei Joe stepped out for dinner and put Keith in charge of the class. It went downhill fast. When Keith began dishing out the pain, one of the elder students with a salt and pepper beard spoke up.

"I'm not here to be your personal punching bag. You need to relax."

"I'm not here to take it easy!" Keith barked. "I'm here to learn. To learn, you must commit completely."

That's all Grey Beard needed to hear. He walked out the door.

Minutes later, I was tossed to the floor with a hip throw that landed me square on my pelvis. I limped to the side to shake it off while Keith continued his onslaught with the rest of the village innocents.

While big Brian and Keith had an aggressive confrontation where Keith wrangled Brian to the floor with a discomforting arm-bar, Sensei Joe strutted in with a look of rage across his face. Apparently Grey Beard, passing Sensei on the street who was sucking the dinner from his teeth, informed him of the shenanigans happening in his dojo. Sensei Joe entered the mat area – steam blasting from his ears – a steely glare from behind his steel-rimmed glasses and in full Buddy Love mode.

"Maybe you'd like to try that on me." He said walking up to Keith.

Keith, having separated himself by taking a few steps to the side, set himself into a loose defensive stance. Sensei Joe invited him to attack by giving him a double handed "c'mere" wave. Nothing more was said. Keith took the challenge without a beat. Within seconds, Keith flashed an attack on Sensei Joe that he was not prepared for… a few quick strikes, which set Sensei back on his heals and surprised.

Sensei Joe was a lethal weapon, but Keith was a certifiable killer. He was a head taller than Sensei, cut from granite… the kind of guy whittled into a lean muscle through inner rage and nervous energy. There was no doubt in my mind this man had killed before and would probably kill again – either on the streets as one of our trusted neighborhood police officers, in our schools as an over-looked Phys-Ed teacher, or in a terrible, dive bar mangling.

Sensei Joe reset himself, seeing that Keith wasn't going to give him a 90% *"attack Sensei Joe at the end of class so he could blow off steam"* mode, but his full-on, 100% *"I'm finally going to show Sensei Joe who the real master is"* mode.

The class stepped back against the wall, the air thick with tension. Sensei attacked, then pulled back. Keith bit on the feign and found himself off-balance. Sensei Joe had a hand on the back of Keith's neck and tossed him to the side. Keith recovered and attacked in full wrestling mode, going for a full-on tackle to Sensei's midsection. Sensei spun away and backpedaled across the room, gaining himself space to reset. Keith met him on the other side, sweat and rage poring off his beet-red face. Another flash attack and before anyone could focus on the flailing arms and legs, Sensei was behind Keith, having wrapped him up and helpless in a chokehold. He slowly back-pedaled Keith into the next room, probably the former dining room, where a heavy bag hung in the middle of the darkened space.

None of us dared even peak around the corner. After some light mumbling where I believe Sensei told Keith to relax, he released his hold and the two entered the training area again yanking on their Gi's and straightening out their hair. Class ended early that day.

I've been around a few bar fights in my day and grew up with the occasional school-yard scuffle, but this was by far the most intense confrontation I'd ever witnessed. Years of animosity and pride laid out in a battle burst that lasted no more than 30 seconds. The energy was both terrifying and electric. Something that either fed or repelled you. It drove me deeper into the training. I soon became obsessed with martial arts, training day and night. I attended class regularly, got a subscription to Black Belt Magazine, read books by and about Bruce Lee, mastered the nunchaku and bo staff, and stretched myself until I could do a split – AKA the full Van Damme. Not only that, but Martial Arts also increased my confidence.

A year later, our dojo would move again to another second floor. This time on the outskirts of town above a deli in a stand-alone building. I saw Keith once more after that, but I believe the confrontation left a bitter taste in his mouth and soon he was gone. Renee was long gone as well. She barely made it into the first year above the flower shop.

Eventually, I was gone as well. After more than three years and on the cusp of receiving my brown belt, I had to quit Sensei Joe's Dojo. I'd emersed myself so deeply into the craft of Jiu Jitsu, I was in danger of failing out of school. My schoolwork consisted of doodles of men cracking one another over the head with fists, and an array of Yin/Yang symbols. My C-minus average fell to a D-minus and if I wasn't careful, I'd be repeating the 11th grade again. When I told Sensei Joe I was leaving, he was gravely disappointed. He felt I had real potential to not only be a great martial artist, but someone who could compete at a high level and maybe even be a competitive champion. The white belt that entered his class three years prior was leaving a dedicated and hardened veteran.

Like my old friend Tony, I eventually crossed over to

Kung Fu too. At first, I studied Wu Shu, which is a traditional flowing, almost dance-like style of the art, then took some classes at a Wing Chun school at Syracuse before studying Jeet Kune Do, the art Bruce Lee created. All in all, I probably dedicated about six years to martial arts.

It's been said the martial arts instils a confidence in the practitioner that comes out in the way they handle themselves. Not cockiness... more like a pillar of passivity. The only real "fight" I ever got into was on Marshall Street at Syracuse, where a mouth-frothing frat guy in a reverse ball cap pointed a red solo cup at me and told me repeatedly he was going to kick my ass. While his friend held him back, my friends sat on the hood of a car and lit cigarettes, curious to see how the scenario unfolded. In a defensive stance, I held out my hand and in a soft manner, repeatedly suggested to frat guy, "I think you should calm down," which only infuriated him more. When his friend noticed my overwhelmingly calm nature, and my friend's desire to sit back and watch the action, he got a realization across his face that maybe it was best for them to move on. Little did he know I was practically shitting my pants, my pulse pounding in my neck. But, he yanked frat guy away and said, "You're lucky we didn't kick your ass" to which I replied in my best Clint Eastwood voice: "I am lucky." That was it. The big showdown.

I have never used martial arts to defend myself in any way, shape, or form in all my years. Certainly not in the streets and never in a school yard with 7-year-olds.

Bruce Lee stated that if you practice your art enough, when it comes time to defend yourself, you don't strike, the fist strikes all by itself. Although I believe I still have the mental mindset to execute the movements, the physical execution is another story. I might be a little rusty these days. If I got into a fight and my fist was to strike all by itself, it would most likely hit me in my own face, knock over my beer… or potentially strike so hard it would pop my arm from the shoulder like a well-boiled chicken leg off the carcass.

The 'Good Ol' Days' of Sports

The science of sports is so advanced these days, a team of quantum engineers is required to fit a jockstrap around the ass of an NFL fullback. The diet of the average athlete is constructed using advanced computers that break down the DNA in bloodwork, and physical performance is analyzed through motion capture generators which can help perfect throwing motions, foot placement, and field vision. Pretty soon we'll just send computers onto the field to test their mettle against robots. It will be like a demolition derby without any human involvement. We can cheer the Cincinnati Cyborgs as they smash the Los Angeles Androids.

Today's American Football players are assassins of their craft. They play *one* position, and they're masters of that domain. We have punters, and place kickers, and even a long snapper who hikes the ball to the holder so the place kicker can kick a field goal. And that's all the long snapper does. Back in the old days... and I mean way back in the 1920s and 1930s, guys like Sammy Baugh would play quarterback, punter, linebacker, then fix the leaky plumbing in the clubhouse. Many of the early footballers were paid scraps and had to do other jobs outside of football. They'd play football on Tuesday and Saturday, then work the docks hauling crates of halibut off cargo ships. They had four concussions a week and drank whiskey to numb the pain.

Today, players are so in-tune with their bodies they sleep in hyperbaric chambers and slip into tubs of ice after the game. If they exhibit even *one* woozy step, they're yanked from the game and dunked into concussion protocol. Back in the 1930s, a fifth of Jack Daniels and a wet rag around the head was good enough for all that ailed ya! A medicinal cigar was administered for clearing the cobwebs as often as a crack of smelling salts under the nose.

In the modern game of American Football, I never understood why we needed two different kickers on the team. They're kickers. They use one leg and kick the football. Can't one guy do two jobs in the game? Punting and place kicking? The roster can only allot 53 men. A large chunk of those roster spots should be offensive linemen. If you protect the quarterback with a wall of beefy men, he'll never get hurt. Maybe knocked around occasionally, but if he's upright the entire season, you'd barely need a backup QB. A team should combine multiple positions into one player. I've been championing this idea for as long as anyone has known me. A team's kicker should be some athletic freak of nature... like, a 6 foot 5 beast who can punt the ball a mile, kick a field goal in driving snow, but also be the backup quarterback, and if necessary, a tight end or the assistant quarterback coach if that coach got knocked out on the sideline or was too drunk to show up for work.

Tom Brady would have never been able to work on the defensive side of the ball in the old days. He would have been killed by halftime – and maybe even killed by halftime if he played on the *offensive* side of the ball in the 1940s. Today, if a defensive player breathes on a quarterback, it's a roughing the passer penalty. Back then, a defensive guy could continue to go after the quarterback long after the ball left the QB's hands. He could run him down like a schoolyard bully and mash him into the ground, then pummel him like a chicken cutlet while the lone ref looked at something unrelated to the game… like the train schedule out of town.

The old school guys had to play two-way. They had no choice. It was in their contract, which paid them about 100 bucks a season. One minute they were the running back, the next, the quarterback, then, back in the game to play defensive linebacker, as well as the backup quarterback. It made no sense, but it's what they did. The teams had 12 to 14 men, so everyone either did double-duty and got back onto the field regardless of their condition. Their fingers were snapped like wicker rods and taped to other fingers blackened and bloodied from trauma. Their noses were permanently pancaked to their cheeks and their eyes off-kilter like Alfred E. Neumann. Look at old photos of Red Grange and Ed Healy. They don the appearance of a five-gallon buckets coated in ground beef and placed on shoulder pads. Their heads could split coconuts and their mouths had fewer teeth than a two-year-old.

The old school players barely wore any protection. Their helmets were leather and an early form of plastic. The helmets had no face masks. Big defensive tackle, Ed Neal would literally slam his fist over Bulldog Turner's head and crack his helmet in half like an ostrich egg. They'd talk to each other across the line of scrimmage and negotiate the terms. Ed Neal would tell center Bulldog Turner that he was "going to punch him in the face" and then do it. Bulldog would ask Neal not to do it again if he himself promised not to hold so much. It was a bizarre system. There were hardly any rules. It made cage fighting seem like a sewing circle. Neal broke Bulldog's nose five times over the course of their rivalry. It got to the point where Bulldog would duck after hiking the ball so he wouldn't be on the receiving end of a knuckle sandwich. The refs didn't do any rule enforcement. They were paid peanuts and had one eye on the clock... and not the game clock, but the "clock out" clock so they could get on with their real jobs, which could be anything from a warehouse manager to a bookie running numbers. These players would tackle a guy to the ground, punch them in the head, then stomp on their guts as they walked away. Today, that would not only be a huge penalty, but an ejection, a fine, and maybe even a short suspension. 1930s football was a gladiator sport. Vicious and mean.

The players of today are tough, no doubt. Incredibly tough. But there was something different about the players back in the day. They had nothing to lose but football games. Bulldog Turner came to the attention of scouts when a photo of him appeared carrying a 400-pound cow across his shoulders. Red Grange once told a story that Bulldog Turner once fell out of a four-story window with a heavy thump and when a policeman ran over shouting, "What's going on around here?" Bulldog, dusting himself off said, "Damned if I know, I just got here myself."

There's a famous picture of Len Dawson smoking a cigarette on the sidelines during Super Bowl II. He's dragging on the butt so hard; you'd think it was oxygen. Football wasn't the refined sport it is today. It was for bruisers and killers. The film North Dallas Forty based on the book by Peter Gent was a fairly realistic portrayal of football in the olden days of the sport. Guys popped pills like candy and smoked weed and cigarettes to numb the crushing pain. Bennies and Goofballs were just as important as a knee brace and pads. Gatorade is a thing of the past in sports. Sure, sugar and salt water is a good shot once in a while, but today's players are sucking down liquids built by lab workers who also design things meant to wipe out the human race like deadly viruses constructed from Bat DNA and mold spores. In the 1930s, while players sat on hard wooden benches in zero degree Ohio weather, a cheek full of tobacco was good enough to replenish your depleted system as much as a swish of electrolyte elixirs.

The players of professional hockey didn't fare any better. Not only did they not wear face protection, they didn't wear helmets at all. Who knew that slapping a hardened rubber puck 120 miles an hour could be dangerous to someone's face? These poor bastards looked like victims of war. Gashes across the scalp and lips like Frankenstein's monster. They skated around on slippery, rock-hard ice while launching pucks at one other like skeet shooting clay pigeons. They checked and tripped each other and knock around like bowling pins. They'd also pound their heads in with their fists until they needed to be dragged off like slaughtered cattle.

Protecting the net was a fool's errand. The goalie was an especially deadly job. They'd stand there naked-faced while men slapped pucks at them, often blocking the net with their skull... their teeth crashing into their throats. It only took 42 years of mandible-mangling, metopic facial splittings before Montreal Canadiens goalie Jacques Plante came up with the idea to wear facial protection in a game, a decision that set the profit margin of the American Dental Society back a few decades. To add insult to injury, he was briefly ridiculed as being a *wussie* because he didn't want his head caved in with pucks!

Today's Hockey players look like the Michelin man. They're wrapped up in so much padding they could tumble down the side of a mountain during an avalanche and walk away unscathed. Back then, players like Stan Mikita would take a stick to the face all game, get stitched between periods while chain-smoking cigarettes, then back out on the ice like he was punching the clock. Who needs functioning lungs when half your head is lying on a bed of ice? Goalie Terry Sawchuk was hit in the face so many times by speeding pucks, his face resembled a stitched catcher's mitt – with the coloring to match.

Speaking of catcher's mitts, the world of baseball wasn't any tamer. Before the days of the big salary, many players were farmers, truckers and ditch diggers. They couldn't add two numbers together, but they played the game like wild animals. It was all they had. Shoeless Joe Jackson was illiterate, but he was known as one of the greatest of all time.

I complain about the amount of specialty players in

today's football (kickers, hikers and holders), but baseball uses about 15 pitchers a game. After the starting pitcher comes out, sometimes in the 6th inning, they parade a mind-numbing train of middle and closing relievers to finish the job. Unfortunately, most stadiums stop serving alcohol after the 7th inning stretch, which is unfortunate because inning 7 though 9 can take longer than all the innings that came before them COMBINED. You need alcohol to kill the time. Some specialty pitchers come in for one inning. Some guys come in for one batter! Of course, each guy needs to warm up his arm by throwing 25 pitches once he runs to the mound, even though he's been throwing in the bullpen for half an hour. Placing and yanking five or six relievers during this timeframe can take hours. It's enough to drive you to drink… unfortunately they stop serving. Such cruelty!

Back in the old days, a guy like Satchel Page pitched till his freakin' arm practically fell off. He'd pitch a full game, go home and eat dinner, then come back and pitch another full game. Page was a freak, but he's also an example of endurance. He threw till his arm was a noodle… chow mein. He threw till his arm was dead and needed to be revived. He played until he was 59, probably because he was paid peanuts… literally. He was a Negro League legend and only started playing in the Major Leagues for the Cleveland Indians at 42. 42! Most guys are done by the time they're 35 – put out to pasture and ready to blow their millions on trucks-loads of dumb crap. Lou Gerhig was the Iron Horse, but perhaps the epithet should have gone to Satchel Page, although his fortitude is a compliment to horses… and maybe iron. Guys today throw a fast ball and 10 minutes later need Tommy John surgery (that's when they take a tendon from somewhere in your body and nail it to your elbow like a rubberband). The only ball Stachel threw was a fastball – thousands and thousands of times. If you took all of Page's throws and strung them together, they'd probably circumference the earth a few dozen times. It's a mind-boggling achievement. They don't build guys like that anymore.

Page was born in 1906, two years before the Model T rolled off the line. Like the footballers, baseballers played the game wherever they could find a field. Lines were painted, bags tossed on the ground and they made a game. They played on dust bowl fields where a slide into second base could form a dirt cloud that lingered for half the inning. They baked in the unforgiving sun and drank beer, and when the game was over, they hopped on a railroad box car whose tracks were most-likely running through the field of play – onto their next playing destination... like a bunch of hobos. Today, players have curfews and are accounted for pretty much day and night. They're taking luxury planes and buses that have the comfort of their living rooms.

Sure, today's players get out to the clubs, but the game is their life. There's no incentive to screw it up. Lost games could be lost revenue and even public shame. Going way back to the turn of the LAST century, a guy like Rube Waddell would leave the stadium in the middle of the game to go fishing. That's understandable as the guy once played for the Chicago Orphans. What did the team to expect? Today's organizations keep tabs on their players by the minute. Waddell would disappear for months. One time the team tracked him down and found him wrestling alligators in a circus. Rube had the attention span of a child. He was known to be distracted in the middle of the game by puppies, fire trucks, as well as shiny objects. It should come as no surprise that Rube had a drinking problem.

Most players of old got through their playing days on drugs and alcohol. They didn't have the benefits of modern science. You know... steroids, HGH and advanced pain killers. Dock Ellis was a notorious drug user and on June 12, 1970, pitched a no-hitter high on acid. Laying on his girlfriend's couch, she reminded him he needed to pitch minutes after he dropped acid. Dock didn't realize that multiple days had passed from his last game as he was caught in the throes of a drug-infused haze. Some will tell you that being high can get you laser-focused. Acid can get you into all kinds of strange headspaces. During the game, while covering first base after a hit, Dock pirouetted around, snagged the ball from first baseman Bob Robertson and landed thinking, "I just scored a touchdown."

Drugs fail players more often than not. Today's players are tested for drugs during the season *constantly* – especially after an incredible game.

Unique characters and skull-crushing violence is not exclusive to baseball and the NFL. Basketball had enough wack jocks to fill a hall of fame and more. Especially the ABA (American Basketball Association). While basketball was solidifying into its current form of popularity, the ABA was a primordial ooze of crazy dysfunction and wild men. Today, players travel together in style on airplanes as cushy as a lazy-boy chair. In the early 70s, players were lucky to get a ride at all. Some were transported in whatever was available, and some were known to hitchhike to games or get rides from strangers. Contemplating his plane ticket one day, Marvin "Bad News" Barnes of the St. Louis Spirits saw that his flight from Louisville at 8:00 a.m. would get into St. Louis at 7:56 a.m. Not understanding the time zones, Marvin told announcer Bob Costas, who would often travel with the team, "I ain't gettin' on no time machine," and instead rented a car and drove to the game. Marvin tried to renegotiate his contract and disappeared until the team tracked him down in a smoky pool hall with his agent.

While NFL guys were clobbering each other over the head like hammers, ABA guys were punching each other in the faces. Warren Jabari of the Oakland Oaks was one of the toughest, nastiest players in the league. In a game against the Los Angeles Stars, Jabari literally stomped on the head of Jim Jarvis as he was running down the court. Jabari raised the ire of everyone in the league. During a game versus the Virginia Squires, Jabari had been knocking the opposing players around like crash dummies. Virginia forward Neil "Enforcer" Johnson, having had enough, came down to the foul line and clocked him the face, knocking him out. Referee John Vanak recalled: "in 28 years of officiating, it was the most devastating punch I'd ever seen on the court." Johnson stood over Jabari shouting for him to get up. Supposedly so he could do it again.

Then there's the infamous Rudy Tomjanovich incident of 1977, when Kermit Washington socked Rudy of the Houston Rockets in the nose during a scuffle with the Los Angeles Lakers. Kermit crushed a piece of nose cartilage into Tomjanovich's skull, causing blood and spinal fluid (ugh) to leak into his head. It was a gruesome incident that got Washington suspended for 60 games. Kareem Abdul Jabbar said the sound was similar to a melon hitting concrete, and the arena fell into "the loudest silence you have ever heard" from the shock of it. The doctor likened the reconstructive surgery to "scotch-taping an eggshell back together."

Today's modern basketball fans won't stand for violence. Both figuratively and literally. The infamous 2004 Malice in the Palace started after crazy Ron Artest pushed Detroit Piston Ben Wallace in the back on a dunk attempt. Double bench-clearing fisticuffs broke out when Artest was doused with a full cup of beer from a spectator, and he stormed into the stands and went after the fans. Players punching each other in the face is one thing, but fans are another. Ron was suspended 73 games and Ben Wallace six. It was a harsh suspension, but necessary as protecting the fans was critical. Players punching players was still frowned upon. But back in the day, a good sock in the nose was not only encouraged, but it could also be lucrative.

Another nut in the ABA days was tough-as-nails John Brisker. Brisker was so nasty that teams would hire thugs just to rough up Brisker in a game. Dallas coach Tom Nissalke, checkbook in hand, told his team, "The first guy in this room who decks Brisker will get $500." Lenny Chappell, who'd never started a game, asked to be put in. As the opening jump ball went into the air, and everyone looked up, Chappell crushed Brisker, laying him out. No one saw Brisker get hit. After the game, Lenny got his $500 and the team won the game.

Legendary fights took place between Brisker and

Wendell Ladner, a hard-nosed bull who resembled actor Burt Reynolds and was beloved by everyone league-wide. Brisker and Ladner had legendary fights on the court. Wendell was a crazy man who played over the top… crashing the boards and into the stands for loose balls. In one game he dove so hard he smashed his face into a glass water cooler, gashing his head open, which required 48 stitches. He wanted to return in the second half to finish the game! In his first matchup with Ladner, Brisker threw a series of elbows until Ladner went nuts and started pounding on him. Before every game of the season between the two bruisers, Ladner would pop his head into the locker room and berate Brisker, asking him, "we going to go at it now, or after the game?"

Today's sports are a field of sophistication. Players don't take chops to the throat at the hands of other players. They ride to games in expensive cars and wear fancy clothes. They're hired guns who can do specialty work in a very specific field… like a plumber who can only loosen nuts and never tighten them. Men can make millions tossing a ball in a hole and nothing more. Of course there's pressure to it… people watching, and championships are on the line. But the guy who can dead-eye shoot a ball from anywhere on the court, may not be able to stop an opposing player from doing the same thing, yet he's still paid in giant sacks of money with those cartoony dollar signs on them.

The football placekicker will never take a meaty fist to the face unless he gets mouthy in a bar full of angry bikers. The only stipulation of his job is to occasionally kick a high-pressure field goal to win the game. Conditions could be windy, or wet, and maybe even powdery white. Yet he will be paid more for one kick than I will in a year, regardless if he makes it or not. The Baltimore Ravens kicker Justin Tucker made $6,000,000 a year for swinging his leg really fast. He had one job and could basically buy an island and live in paradise while creating generational wealth while I struggle to buy meat softer than a leather shoe, and I do about 15 jobs at my job. None of which require me to kick anything, unless it's the garbage can when something goes terribly wrong. But that's a voluntary act. It's not in my job description. But apparently neither is tackling for the kicker, and once in a while the kicker is required to do *just that*, and watching a professional kicker try and tackle a player storming down field because they scooped up the kickers wonky kick is nothing short of shameful. Mainly because he'll be tossed aside like a cat on a carousel when said player plows through the kicker's single-bar facemask like a locomotive.

Chase Daniels was a backup quarterback his entire career and made a whopping 42 million bucks. He's started only five games in his entire career. FIVE! That's about 8.5 million per start. Unbelievable. Two-way playing legends like Chuck "Concrete Charlie" Bednarik made a pittance in relation to that salary and is considered one of the greats of all time. Concrete Charlie clotheslined Frank Gifford so hard he knocked him out of the game… for 18 months! He called today's players pussyfoots who "couldn't tackle my wife Emma." Even feared legend Dick Butkus didn't make as much money as Daniels and fell back on B-grade films like *Hamburger: The Motion Picture*… which, I must admit, is one of the best Tits and Ass movies of the 1980s. Maybe check it out. It was brilliant when I was 14. Butkus wasn't exactly executing Academy-Award winning material here. His pay versus value of play compared to today is all out of whack.

Jerry Jones, owner of the Dallas Cowboys built a stadium that cost 1.4 billion dollars and the So-Fi Stadium in Los Angeles cost a jaw-dropping 5 billion dollars. Both have giant TV screens wrapping around the stadium that are bigger than stadiums built before the year 2000. In 1925, Charlie C.C. (Cash & Carry) Pyle once hired 200 carpenters to quickly build a wooden stadium in the middle of a field in Coral Gables, Florida. Star Red Grange and the Chicago Bears played a game in a stadium where two days before there was nothing but mud. The next day the stadium was torn down and the field looked as if nothing had ever been there.

The salaries of sports stars are going up while the average salary of the common worker is dropping. You need two week's pay for a family of four to see a game, and if you want them to eat, well, prepare to mortgage the house. The old days are long gone, and the new days are here... that's for sure. Offense is offense and defense is defense. The game of football is violent, and basketball has the occasional scuffle, but you certainly won't see a punch to the face that causes a nose to explode, or the ground littered with teeth from a hockey puck to the grill.

Were the good old days of sports *better* or just primitive and different? Are we seeing the finest product from elite athletes with associated costs, or is everything out of whack?

I can't truly say, but I do know this... I wouldn't mind seeing a player crack another guy's helmet in half with his fist while I eat a 5-cent hotdog.

REFERENCES:

The Football Book – Sports Illustrated – Rob Fleder

The Game that Was – Myron Cope

Loose Balls – Terry Prachett

Dock Ellis & The LSD No-No – James Blagden

Concrete Charlie – John Schulian

Paper Lion – George Plimpton

Bleacher Report

Wikepedia

I may have gotten some of the information confused during my research. If that's the case, I apologize, but truthfully, I don't give a shit… just like in the good ol' days. Or is that a new thing?

A Super Bowl Guide
for Beginners

If you don't know anything about the Super Bowl, no problem! This guide will help you navigate the Xs and Os of Super Bowl Sunday; and I don't mean hugs and kisses. That's a different kind of game... a psychological love game that is far more complicated than the game of football. Xs and Os in football represent Offense and Defense. But love can be like that too if you think about it – an offense and a defense.

But let's not get distracted. I'm about to penetrate a line I shouldn't cross. That's a double entendre that will be *way* funnier later for those unfamiliar with the game of football... or love.

This guide is about the game of football itself, particularly the Super Bowl – the championship game that culminates after months and years of backbreaking labor, bone-breaking injuries, and hours and hours of inner turmoil. I'm talking about the fans. The players are being paid millions of dollars and accumulating generational wealth. They deserve very little of our sympathy.

By the end of this guide, you will not only be informed, but enlightened. This guide will:

1. educate you in the nuances of American Football;
2. help you navigate any Super Bowl party you're invited to;
3. help temper any problem areas you have with partygoers heavily involved in the sport;
4. even help you enjoy the game.

Let's get started... shall we?

PART I: Introduction

First and foremost, don't pretend you've never heard of the Super Bowl. Even someone living in the woods for five decades in a different country has heard of the Super Bowl. If you intend to use the term "sports ball game" as a snarky reference to any sport, especially a championship, please stay at home and stare at the wall. Even the most welcoming, liberal, fun-loving sports fan will be tempted to kick you in the nuts – even if you're a woman. We get it, you don't watch football. It's fine. People will not be angry with you for not watching or knowing anything about the game. But coming to an event in which you're openly hostile to its culture will not ingratiate you to others. It's the equivalent of going to a book reading and shouting: "all they did was stick a bunch of words together! What's the big deal?"

Second, whether you're at a Super Bowl party with a small group of friends or at a raging bash, it helps to drink alcohol. If you don't drink, smoke some marijuana. If you don't smoke, try cocaine, meth or in a pinch… heroin. If you don't do drugs, eat shitty food like chicken wings coated in drippy sauces, cheeseburgers layered with bacon, or hot dogs loaded with chili. If you don't eat meat, try the vegetarian alternatives. If you're not into any of these things, consider your life choices. You may be incredibly boring. I mean; what do you do? Do you masturbate? skydive? Breed cactuses? Does your heart rate rise *at all?* Do you have a pulse? Please review and get back to this guide when you know.

NOTE: I don't support the use of drugs. They're terrible for you and will destroy your life. What you do with bacon and your private parts is up to you.

Third, if you've never been to a party before, don't fret… a Super Bowl party is the best introduction to a party possible. Having never been to a party in your natural born life is a different situation entirely. That's a discussion to have with your therapist, clergyman or your local street bum.

Super Bowl parties have absolutely no formality whatsoever, other than the golden party rule, which is: "if you're going to a party you've been invited to, bring something." Beer is a no brainer. You could bring chips, dips, guacamole, or any kind of snack, but it's best to keep things simple. Another great thing about going to a Super Bowl party is the host rarely cares if you were invited by them or not. Unless you're the host's ex-lover, currently under the restrictions of a restraining order initiated by someone in attendance, or going to jail for murder, you will be welcome with open arms. As long as you are willing to listen to people shout at the TV, spill food on themselves, get wildly drunk, and fall on the floor at your feet (and perhaps have someone unattractive hit on you) then you'll be right at home. Mi casa, su casa… that type of philosophy. Open the fridge, grab a beer, sit down, and enjoy.

Finally, it helps to have a general idea about the rules of the game. That's what this guide is for!

PART II: Rules of the game

Think of the football game as a battlefield of armies. Men instinctually want to kill each other whether it's actually on a battlefield or vicariously through sports, so consider football a healthy outlet.

One army (team) is on one side of the field, the other team is on the other side. There's no guns, knives or swords. That's at middle school games. Pro games have no weapons other than the security who've made sure no one has weapons. Now, one TEAM is trying to take over the other team's castle (so to speak) by scoring a TOUCHDOWN in the END ZONE (the end section of the field with a team logo in it).

They can accomplish that by either throwing the ball to a receiver in the end zone, or running the ball with a running back into the end zone. The other team is trying to defend that from happening. Then, the other team gets the ball and tries to do the same. Easy enough, yes?

Here's the thing (you knew this would get complicated) … the team that is trying to score (the offense) has only FOUR chances to move the ball TEN yards. If they do, they get a new set of four chances (called DOWNS) to do it again. This is where drinking alcohol comes in handy. Consider it.

Now, let's do some math, shall we?

It is now '1st down and 10 yards to go' (usually abbreviated to 1st and 10). Meaning: it's the 1st opportunity for the offense to go 10 yards for another first down. The Quarterback, that's the screaming guy in the middle with his hands between the center's legs (the center being the big guy bent over with his hand on the ball on the ground), has the ball HIKED (handed) to him and he, the quarterback, then hands the ball to the running back who runs the ball five yards until he is tackled to the ground. It is now:

A. 2nd and 5

B 1st and 5

C. 1st and 10

D. I have no idea.

If you chose A, you'd be correct! Because the NEXT play will be the second opportunity to take the ball another 5 yards to get a new set of downs.

See? It's not that hard. If you chose D, please consider drinking more or taking mild drugs.

GAME NOTE: Yes, when the quarterback has his hands between the center's legs, he's probably touching the center's nut sack, but that's not important right now. You could bring that up to someone in the room to get an "interesting" conversation going, but that is at your discretion.

Here's another fun prompt you could toss out during

the game to get a "fun" conversation going whether you understand what you're talking about or not:

• Asking "What's the spread?" No, this isn't about how far the Center can part his legs for the Quarterback's hands. Nor is this about the food laid out on the table. You should have snooped that already. The SPREAD is in reference to gambling. It's what the Las Vegas odds makers have predicted MIGHT be the number of points one team scores over the other, or in conjunction, what the combined score of the two teams will be in total, which is called the OVER/UNDER. You'll hear a shit load of numbers being thrown around. Pay no attention to them. They're meaningless. Just enjoy your beverage and if people start slapping money on a table, say you don't gamble, and no one will judge you.

Let's get back to football rules.

We'll continue with the down and distance thing... let's say it's 4th and 7. That means the offense must go (at least) seven yards to get a fresh set of downs. If they don't do that on the 4th try, they turn the ball over to the other team on the spot they fail to convert the first down.

Depending on where the offense is on the field, they may choose to either:
1. punt the ball to the other team and let them have a go of attacking their end zone (castle) or;
2. if they are close to the other team's end zone, but afraid of not scoring a touchdown or getting the first down, they

can kick a field goal. A field goal is when the kicker, a man who does nothing but kick a football for millions of dollars a season, tries to kick the ball between those giant yellow sticks (GOAL POSTS). That's 3 points.

A Touchdown is 6 points. When a touchdown is scored, the team that scores can convert an extra point by having that millionaire kicker guy run onto the field and kick one through the tall goal posts for 1 extra point; or the team can try and essentially score another touchdown for two points (called a two-point conversion) starting from the defender's two-yard line. They only get one shot at the two-point conversion. That's it! That's the whole freakin' game. The only other way for a team to score is if the defense:

1. causes a fumble (makes the offense drop the football), scoops it up and runs it into the end zone for a touchdown;
2. gets an interception (catches the other team's pass) and runs it into the end zone, or;
3. gets a SAFETY, which is two points. A safety is when the defense has the offense pinned back inside the walls of their own castle (end zone) and tackles a man (usually the quarterback) in the castle before he can leave it.

There's many, many more fascinating aspects to the game. In fact, American football gets so complicated, even the coaches and players don't know all the rules; and football is what they do for a living!

This is a good start to enjoying any Super Bowl game you're watching on TV. Certain aspects of the party you can figure out yourself. Things like flirting, chip and dip etiquette, alcohol tolerance, pop culture, and geography are all things you should have learned or figured out ages ago.

But, since this is a guide to the Super Bowl as an experience, let's make you an expert. Here's some things that may pop up during the festivities that are exclusive to the Super Bowl.

PART III: Party Games

• A Super Bowl Pool: No, this is not the kind of pool with water, although if you live in an area where the weather is warm year-round, you could end up in the swimming pool. I mean, there's alcohol at these parties, so you never know.

A Super Bowl Pool is a large chart on the wall with 100 boxes. People enter by giving the pool runner some money (usually $20) and then, they give you a pen to write your name in one of the available boxes. Later, numbers are drawn, and each row and column receives a number, and if the game score ends with two numbers that align with your box, you win some cash. If you don't understand, don't worry about it. By the end of the night, someone either hands you some cash or doesn't. The pool is especially good for people who know absolutely nothing about football because they're usually the winner. It's like the person who knows absolutely nothing about college basketball, yet their bracket is perfect right through to the championship game because that's just the way life is. Beginner's luck.

If you've already stated you don't gamble but want to play, just say "oh, this is just for fun!" If you believe you may need to say you don't gamble later in the party, be prepared to state you have a gambling problem and people will drop all gambling talk and may even drift away. I'm not sure why, but gambling is a mysterious addiction that most people don't handle well upon hearing.

• Super Bowl Party People Watching: This activity is not only fun, but fascinating. You can learn a lot about society by scrutinizing humans in excitable sports moments, but more specifically, in quieter moments when their team is losing. Since most people are glued to the TV on Super Bowl Sunday, you can freely stare at your fellow party goers to observe who's a major asshole and who has friend potential. You can also categorize people if that's how your brain works. You can locate:

–The Scout: Know-it-all who seems to know WAY too much about football. Even where the players went to college.

–The TKO: That's the guy who's so bombed, he's drifting off to sleep because he started drinking at 8am.

–The Sun: The person most people revolve around (not Super Bowl exclusive).

–The Comedy Assassin: The person who says one thing that busts up a room, then says nothing for 10 minutes. Not a clown. Not a wallflower.

–The Refrigerator Magnets: A subsection of people who linger in the kitchen. Kitchens are warm, inviting places. Sometimes they snag hors d'oeuvres fresh from the oven.

–The Stick and Move Man: The guy on the phone, seemingly at another party, but doing it through telecommunication services. Often in and out of the room, and occasionally outside for a cigarette.

–The Superb Owls: The grouping of people who are bookish or non-sporty who know nothing about the Super Bowl or sports. They're wide-eyed and look lost until they find one another.

–The Mystery Guest: Someone completely compelling in many ways. Maybe they're decades older than the rest of the attendees; have a very distinct, unidentifiable accent; or someone wearing clothing or acting as if from a different time or dimension.

–The Controller: That's the person adjusting the volume on the TV because the commercials are usually 5 times louder than the game. Occasionally they'll hit mute for major drink spill or an ash dropping off a flaming joint. At a regular party, they'd be the "DJ."

–The Shot Girl: Regardless of their gender, that's the person roaming the party sticking shots of alcohol in everyone's face because they want to "get the party started."

Now, if you'd like more advanced knowledge on

football, please keep reading. You may find nuances to the game you never thought possible.

PART IV: The Other Side of the Ball

Let's continue with De-fense!

Thwarting the advances of a drunken party goer is not always easy... wait. That's a different type of defense. Part of that non-football X and O thing. We can get to that later... right now this is all football.

One of the main aspects of defense, besides stopping the offense from scoring, is the honorable pursuit of trying to kill the other team's quarterback. Ever since the quarterback position was invented, there's been someone on the other side of the ball trying to stomp that fucker into the ground.

When a PASS RUSHER (defensive player putting pressure on the offense) penetrates the LINE OF SCRIMMAGE (that's the imaginary line, kind of like the equator, where the ball lies) and gets into the BACKFIELD (that's where the quarterback and running back are hanging out) and crushes the quarterback for a loss, it's called a SACK. You may find that a sack is just as, if not *more* satisfying, than a touchdown.

Enjoying sacks reveals something about a person. If you're the special kind of someone who enjoys watching quarterbacks mauled like a bear, you may have the potential to be a serial killer or the CEO of a large Fortune 500 company. When a sack occurs, if your team is the one crushing the QB, feel free to stand and shout, "Yeah, take that mother fucker," point to the TV, and high-five the person nearest you.

I know what you're thinking: "High fives are stupid backwards-ball-cap-bro bullshit," but believe me, after an awesome sack, regardless if you're a 250-pound power lifter or a 90-pound ballerina, turning to someone and connecting on a solid high five (with satisfying clap noise) is as close to Zen as you're likely to get sitting on a couch watching TV.

When a sack occurs, it usually means the offense lost yards. So, (test time!) if the defense knocks the QB back 10 yards on the FIRST play of the drive, it will now be...?

A. 1st and 20
B. 1st and 10
C. 2nd and 20
D. 4th and 7

If you said C, you'd be correct. Any other answer means you should start hard drugs and re-reading this entire chapter again. This isn't trigonometry we're doing here. Like I said before, I don't support drug use, but you're struggling.

The huge defensive linemen near the line of scrimmage are trying to get to the QB while also stopping the run. The players more in the back of the defensive line are LINEBACKERS and they try and stop the receivers and the runners, and the guys way in the back are CORNERBACKS and SAFETIES and they're trying to stop the receivers. The RECEIVERS are the tall, thin guys from the offense who are running around trying to avoid the defensive so they can catch the ball.

Since we're discussing positions, let's talk about players and terminology you may hear on TV and from the people at the party who are screaming at the TV.

PART V: Game Terminology

TIGHT END: I get it. The number of jokes you could make about this position are endless. The tight end (an offensive player) is one of the more versatile players on the field. A good tight end can line up to block defensive players, go out for passes, or carry the ball like a running back. In relation to chess, he's sort of like the versatile queen (pairing queen and tight end in one sentence is dangerous), but he's also like the knight piece as well. If you know nothing about chess, I'm sorry, my chapter about chess has yet to be written.

ZEBRA: That's a derogatory term for the referees who are wearing black and white stripes. You'll see them on the TV rubbing their bellies and tapping their heads, much like that game people play to see if they can do both things simultaneously. That's the refs alerting you and the crowd what penalty just occurred. If a game is going poorly, you'll see them *way* too often on screen, much to the chagrin of everyone watching whether it affects their team or not. That's because penalties slow the game down and no one wants to see the refs. Penalties include mind-numbing nomenclature like: pass interference, roughing the passer, illegal shift, false start, and offsides. Some are self-explanatory like: too many men on the field, holding, and unnecessary roughness. Even though football is a violent game, there comes a point where some maniac gets so aggressive they need to be called out for their brutality.

BLITZ: that's when the defense, smelling blood in the water like sharks, has the offense on their heels and decides most of the team is going to attack the quarterback at once. A *blitzkrieg*. This is when football is really like a battle. The offense must hold the line like a castle wall, and the quarterback must be quick to either escape or toss the ball to a receiver. Again, if you enjoy seeing quarterbacks mashed into mulch, this is when it's most likely to happen.

CATCH: I know what you're thinking... "I know what a catch is!" And you'd be right, but in this game you'd be wrong. That's because for some reason, a legitimate catch in a football game requires a certain number of factors to happen to call it a catch... some of those criteria changing from game to game. Mainly, the receiver must have both feet INBOUNDS (inside the FIELD of PLAY) for it to be a catch. Easy enough. But the receiver must also have control of the ball (not fumbling around with it) as he is either stepping or being pushed out of bounds. Okay, sure... fine. But, the receiver must ALSO hold onto the ball securely if he falls inbounds, and also hits the ground out of bounds (outside the field of play) if his feet were initially inbounds. I know, it's a bit confusing, but not absurd. The receiver must also make a "football" move for it to be considered a catch. Huh? Yeah. So, for example, our tight end... you can imagine him with a tight end if it helps you... he runs five yards out and catches a pass from the quarterback and a defender knocks it out of his hand. Was it a catch? Well, it depends on what our tight end did. If the ball hit his hands for a second and then was knocked out, it's not really a catch. If he turned and took a step and then it was knocked out, it may be a catch, but we're not sure. It's up to the referees to look at a replay 15 times in slow motion to decide if he made a football move. When the refs are trying to figure this out by looking into a little monitor under a tarp (which is like a little voting booth) you know it's the perfect time to go to the bar and refresh your drink or whatever you're enjoying at that time.

Although watching football seems like a fun activity for those watching the game, it's mostly a frustrating sport. Even though there's levels of enthusiasm, you'll notice most of that enthusiasm is people complaining. Here's some of the more obvious things connoisseurs of the game may be complaining about while watching the game.

PART VI: On the TV

1. The Announcers: Most of the time, there's two announcers doing the game. One guy, usually with a very distinct voice, is sort of the host, but he's also the play-by-play man. He's telling the viewer what is literally happening on screen – as if he's describing the game to a blind person. The other guy, usually a former player, is the color commentator. He's droning on and on about the technical aspects of the game… what the quarterback is seeing on field, what the defense is trying to accomplish, maybe analyzing the last play. Sometimes the networks pair two guys who are like bread and butter, and listening to the two banter is like listening to a

symphony of ear massages – pure magic. Sometimes they pair two guys where one, and sometimes both announcers have the chemistry of a divorced couple arguing at a school play, and it sounds like someone punching your eardrums in the face.

2. The number of commercials current and former athletes appear in. Commercials are part of watching sports more than ever. That's because the NFL must fund the outrageous salaries of today's players. There's a million commercials! Especially during the Super Bowl. In fact, many people now watch the big game for the commercials alone. It's become a cultural phenomenon. Companies spend feature-length movie budgets on these commercials. The ad space alone can bankrupt a small nation, so the commercials are made with extreme care, created by the best ad firms in the field using high-priced writers. That's why they all suck. Usually about 20% of these commercials feature the best current and former quarterbacks, as well as other personable players, and the commercials are so frequent, it feels traumatic.

3. The Referees: Please see above in the Zebra section.

4. The Half Time Show. This is always more about the act and how it impacts all of us culturally. That's because there's three factions of NFL fans to cater to creatively and they don't always cross over. There's the youth and open-minded fans who like all music and will be entertained by rap, hip hop, rock, pop, soul, and even a little country if the act is right; there's the conservative (older) crowd who likes

rock, mostly classic rock, and will only like the show if they recognize songs and can play air guitar to those songs; and then there's country music fans… enough said. Someone is bound to complain about the act regardless. Put out the hottest young soul act who'll light the place on fire and people will complain about skin-tight outfits. Stick an old classic rock act at mid-field averaging 70 years old and people will complain about relevance; and put a country music act out and everyone who hates country will simply complain.

Enough about football and everything that is happening on the Television. Let's go back to the party itself.

PART VII: Party Cautions

Here are some things to avoid at a party:

1. Asking a lot of questions about the rules of the game: That's the point of this guide. But if you've forgotten everything stated once you've gotten to the party, no worries. This might be an opportunity to find a mate. If you find someone attractive at the party, go up and ask them about the rules in the most seductive voice you can muster. Perhaps, it's best to toss out a little knowledge you learned from this guide to impress that person, but not enough so they become argumentative with you.

2. Sitting in the middle of the couch. If you see a lot of people at the party and see an empty couch – beware. If you plop yourself down, there's a good chance everyone split to re-

fresh their drinks and will suddenly return. You could find yourself sandwiched between a crush of sweaty men. If you do need to leave this stifling situation, you need to wait for a break in the game action, which is simple because they show a commercial every 30 seconds.

NOTE: If you get stuck for an extended period in this situation and you're unable to escape, simply stand and ask if anyone needs anything from the bar. Not only can you escape, but you'll quietly become a hero. Not only that, being a waiter is kind of fun, especially if you have social anxiety because now you're on a mission, and that occupies your internal turmoil motor, and no one will argue if you walk into people's game view accidentally.

3. Being a fan of a team people hate. It's fun to be a part of a group. There's community and comfort in knowing someone shares your joy and pain. But rooting for a team that is universally hated leads to a lot of arguing and if you're trying to blend in at the party, avoid rooting for the Dallas Cowboys and the New England Patriots. Those teams are consistently on the list of universally disliked teams. Yes, Dallas is considered "America's Team" and the Patriots won 155 Super Bowls, but the only team that has been a consistent winner while also remaining "down to earth" is the Pittsburgh Steelers. They're a blue-collar team with blue-collar fans. Still, even they ruffle a few feathers. Same with the Green Bay Packers. The best team to root for that is blue collar, is from a small market, and is often fun to watch while still gaining sympathy from other fan bases

because of their lack of Super Bowl wins is the Buffalo Bills. You could root for other sad sack franchises like the Cleveland Browns, or my terrible team, the New York Jets, but that may invite scorn because most fans love to bully the Browns and Jets at this point because they're so goddamn pitiful.

Advanced Party game play:

If you really want to go in deep with the football nerds, locate one of the offensive coordinators on the TV (perhaps the team winning) and ask: "You think he'll be back next year?" Other teams love to pilfer offensive coordinators to make them their coach, especially (obviously) now that they got their team to the Super Bowl. You may not care about the answer, but you'll have engaged with humans and that's a good thing.

PART VIII: Final Random Party Tips

1. Ordering takeout: Even though the place is packed with food, someone will want to get takeout. Be cautious getting involved. Never agree to a "I'll buy if you fly" agreement. That means they're paying for your food, but also paying for you to go to the takeout place. It's rarely a good deal. If people pile money on the table and you do as well, you're absolutely NOT getting any change back, so expect to pay $20 for one slice of pizza. If money (and food choice) is no object, toss in a $20 and say, "I'll have what you're having." If you're waiting for an app delivery order on Super

Bowl Sunday, expect to wait forever.

2. Beware of the 'after the game' show: No, I'm not talking about a sports recap show with the shouting talking head commentators, I'm talking about the show the network is DYING to spoon-feed a massive audience because they feel they have the next best show since Cheers and Seinfeld. Don't get caught in this hypnosis. Turn away and leave before it's too late.

3. Irish goodbyes: If you're not familiar with the controversial Irish goodbye, that's when you leave a party without saying goodbye to anyone – you just bolt. I'm not sure why they call it that, maybe it has something to do with drunkenness, but I prefer it over the regular goodbye. Trust me, half the people won't notice you're gone because they're bombed out of their gourds, and, unless you're ridiculously attractive, half won't remember you at all. So, it's best to just split so you won't spend half an hour reconnecting with every knucklehead in the place, shaking their hands, and wishing them the best of luck in whatever the hell they're going to do with the rest of their lives.

4. Don't drink and drive!

I hope you found this guide informative. Please feel free to read it every year. Pass it along to those who may need it. May the best team win.